The Community Teacher

The Community Teacher

A NEW FRAMEWORK FOR EFFECTIVE URBAN TEACHING

Peter C. Murrell, Jr.

TEACHERS COLLEGE PRESS

Teachers College, Columbia University
New York and London

Published by Teachers College Press, 1234 Amsterdam Avenue, New York, NY 10027

Library of Congress Cataloging-in-Publication Data

Murrell, Peter C.
    The community teacher : a new framework for effective urban teaching / Peter C. Murrell, Jr.
        p.   cm.
    Includes bibliographical references and index.
    ISBN 0-8077-4139-6 (cloth : alk. paper)—ISBN 0-8077-4138-8 (pbk. : alk. paper)
    1. Teachers—Training of—United States.   2. Teachers—In-service training—United States.   3. Education, Urban—United States.   I. Title

    LB1715 .M79   2001
    370'.71'55—dc21   2001027535

ISBN 0-8077-4138-8 (paper)
ISBN 0-8077-4139-6 (cloth)

Printed on acid-free paper
Manufactured in the United States of America

08   07   06   05   04   03   02   01   8   7   6   5   4   3   2   1

To my father, Dr. Peter C. Murrell, Sr.,
and my mother, Eva Ruth Greenlee Murrell

Contents

Introduction

EDUCATION FOR CHILDREN AND YOUTH in our nation's urban schools and communities is in a continuing state of crisis. Children and youth of color, especially African American and Hispanic learners in urban school districts, continue to bear the brunt of public school dysfunction. We live in an era in which educational policy seeks to "raise the bar" under the banners of "raising standards" and "professionalization of teaching," while at the same time tolerating systems of urban schooling that literally throw away children's educational futures.

The national response to the crisis has been a systematic program of increased professionalization of teachers, teacher preparation, and performance-based licensure. Since the 1996 publication of the report of the National Commission on Teaching and America's Future (NCTAF), teacher quality and accountability have moved to center stage in the formulation of school reform nationally, regionally, and locally. A standards-based reform movement for elevating student achievement drives this focus on teacher quality. The *standards* movement translates into an *accountability* movement regarding teacher quality. Against this backdrop is the continuing crisis in urban public education. Urban public schools are where most students go, and most of these students are African American and Hispanic.

In spite of the new national agenda for the professionalization and improvement of teaching, this country has yet to produce a system of teacher education that successfully, and in sufficient numbers, prepares teachers for effective work in diverse urban school settings (Darling-Hammond, 1994; Melnick & Zeichner, 1997; Murrell, 1991, 1997, 1998; NCTAF, 1996; Zeichner, 1996). The challenges for addressing critical issues of diversity have been articulated at the early stages of this new national agenda as three unmet needs by Williams (1999). The first is the need to comprehend and accept the paradigm shift in *conceptualizations of diversity* supported by new understandings of human development. The educational literature has long acknowledged the significance of culturally relevant pedagogy, but there has not yet been a significant impact of this concept on the preparation of teachers nationwide.

1

The second need is to put the new diversity-related understandings about human development at the center of reform proposals designed to increase the learning success of diverse student populations. Urban educational reform is still dominated by the embrace of large-scale, high-stakes standardized testing that neither reflects nor seeks to enrich the intellectual, social, or cultural potential of children of color in diverse urban communities. The third need is to integrate available models and systems of practice for preparing students for successful participation in adult life. These three things—diversity-embedded new understandings of human development, the central positioning of these understandings in reform proposals, and the development of diversity—appropriate models of practice—are the missing pieces in the educational reform landscape.

It has become abundantly clear that the current configurations of teacher education are not yet equipped to fulfill these three needs for renewing urban education (cf. Comer, 1997; Delpit, 1996; Irvine & Fraser, 1998; Hollins, King, & Hayman, 1994; Labaree & Pallas, 1996; Murrell, 1998; Myers, 1996a; Sykes, 1997). Although there is a general consensus that the renewal of teacher preparation will require the bridging of at least two types of professional communities—the community of schools, colleges, and departments of education (SCDEs) on one hand, and school personnel on the other hand—the picture is still incomplete.

It is my contention that a third community of "players" is essential to the renewal of teacher preparation, teacher quality, and school renewal. This is the community of adults who work with children in urban neighborhoods and centers of youth development. The most significant benefit of this partnership with urban communities is the opportunity for schools of education to draw on locally derived practical knowledge in order to develop vital, urban-focused, and community-committed teaching practices. Hence, a key component of the new national agenda is collaboration among institutions of higher education, the K–12 schools they work with, and a broad community constituency. The success of urban school reform will depend, in part, on how the new national agenda makes good on its enthusiasm for creating new "communities of learning," embracing diversity, and preparing teachers through community and collaborative partnership.

A NEW FRAMEWORK FOR EDUCATING
URBAN TEACHERS

This book reconceptualizes the enterprise of teacher education as it relates both to effective practice in urban public schools and to the new national agenda for teacher quality in educational reform. It proposes a new system of practice for urban teacher preparation that produces the professional knowledge essential for effective work with children and youth in diverse urban schools and neighborhoods. It is the fuller articulation of the theoretical and programmatic framework introduced in the monograph *Like Stone Soup: The Role of the Professional Development School in the Renewal of Urban Schools* (Murrell, 1998), which offered a system of practice requiring conjoint collaboration of universities, communities, and schools.

Presented in these pages is a framework for a community-dedicated, research-focused, collaboration-oriented program of urban teacher education. The framework includes an explanation of the relevant theory and illustrates the systems of practice that are essential for the development of a new kind of teacher for effective urban teaching—the *community teacher*. This volume articulates the theoretical and programmatic framework for the preparation of exemplary urban teachers. The book also provides illustrations and examples of the framework as a system of practice. Case examples are used to illustrate the program features necessary for generating the knowledge, skills, and proficiencies required for meeting the demands of effective teaching practice in urban schools, communities, and neighborhoods.

The questions this book addresses are:

1. What constitutes effective practice in today's diverse urban classrooms and communities?
2. What does it take to become an effective urban teacher?
3. What is the trajectory of development from novice to accomplished teaching practice?
4. What systems of inquiry, collaboration, teaching, and professional development produce the accomplished teacher in urban teaching?

The system of teacher education in this volume, which is based on university–community–school partnership, shows how collaborative practice and systemic partnerships should be understood as *ecosocial systems* for developing accomplished practice for both novice and experienced teachers. The framework also shows how research and development in urban teaching can become an integral part of school and university practices designed to enhance the learning achievement of children in urban schools and communities. The framework also couples preservice teacher preparation with professional development, based on the idea that accomplished teaching is a matter of both individual pedagogical knowledge and the capacity to learn, teach, and produce new knowledge in collaboration with others.

The components of the university–community–school partnership framework presented in these pages are also illustrated by case examples drawn from actual experiences involving this work. The cases illustrate the complexity of the issues as well as successful application of key ideas in the framework. The vision of the *community teacher* in the framework guides the development of collaborative partnerships as urban-focused, community-oriented professional development schools. The notion of the *community of practice* is the component that will help illustrate how programs can be synchronized with the new national agenda for teacher quality without sacrificing the development of community-committed, urban-focused, and activity-based systems of practice for teaching in urban schools and communities. The concept of the *circle of practice* is instrumental in showing how teacher preparation programs can move from their traditional arrangements to community-responsive and urban-focused programs.

The volume develops the concept of the *community teacher*. The concept describes both a pedagogical theory of teacher preparation and a program for producing the kind of accomplished urban teachers required to promote learning achievement for children in underresourced urban communities. The notion of the community teacher is at the center of this practice-oriented theory of teacher effectiveness based on a synthesis of the new national agenda's formulations of teacher subject-matter and pedagogical knowledge, student achievement and development, and the induction of competence through field experience.

The term *community teacher* denotes the accomplished practitioner in urban teaching and learning. Community teachers draw on a richly contextualized knowledge of culture, community, and identity in their professional work with children and families in diverse urban communities. Their competence is evidenced by effective pedagogy in diverse community settings, student achievement, and community affirmation and acknowledgment of their performance. Community teachers have a clear sense of their own cultural, political, and racial identities in relation to the children and families they hope to serve. This sense allows them to play a central role in the successful development and education of their students.

This volume targets the crisis of knowledge that currently exists in teacher preparation. State and federal governments have placed rigorous new requirements on teacher preparation. Unfortunately, we lack the knowledge necessary to meet those requirements. As many have observed (e.g., Darling-Hammond & Sykes, 1999), policy makers, professional organizations, and administrators in school departments are too far removed from the local settings of practice to develop a working understanding of the requirements of and constraints on urban teaching and learning. Thus, there is a major gulf between the *proposing* of policy makers and the *doing* of practitioners. It is not that the new national agenda—which seeks to reform schools through the elevation of teaching quality and the professionalization of teachers—is misguided. As stated earlier, the issue is the dearth of practical knowledge about how to implement that agenda.

reform agenda.

This book is about how to design systems that can generate the knowledge base of practical know-how we need to truly accomplish a reform agenda. In this volume I confront the current crisis of knowledge in two ways. First, I provide a blueprint for renewing urban education through the organization of *schools as communities of practice*. I offer a design for a new *system of practice* that connects the work of teacher development and the preparation of urban teachers to higher levels of student achievement. Second, recognizing that a major share of the knowledge needed to improve our schools lies outside the parameters of the typical university, I provide a set of conceptual tools for transforming traditional teacher preparation into successful systems of practice as university–community–school partnerships. This system illustrates the nature of the successful collaboration of university, community, and school partners for meeting the conjoint aims of improving schooling practices and teacher education. To familiarize the reader with the system of practice developed in this book, I briefly outline seven principles of the *community teacher framework*.

PRINCIPLES OF COMMUNITY TEACHER FRAMEWORK

PRINCIPLE ONE

The primary goal of any school of education dedicated to preparing successful and competent urban teachers is the development of a system of accomplished practice. The idea of *accomplished practice* is central to the framework provided in this book. For the present, the best way to think of accomplished practice is as an *activity system:* the composite of professional activities employed by teachers who are successful in promoting the academic achievement and personal development of diverse learners in urban contexts. As an activity system, *accomplished practice* thus includes all professional and instructional activities (e.g., decision making; planning; implementing instruction; interacting interpersonally with students, colleagues, and parents) that facilitate student achievement.

PRINCIPLE TWO

Accomplished practice in diverse urban schools and communities can be articulated, shared, and communicated as a set of standards that make it possible for both practicing teachers and teacher candidates to achieve this level of practice. Accomplished practice means successful work with diverse populations of students in urban public schools—particularly with African American and Hispanic children, who constitute the largest proportion of students in urban school districts. It includes a range of cultural, pedagogical, developmental, and historical understandings that result in the demonstrable growth in students. One of the tasks of an urban-focused, community-dedicated, and practice-oriented program of teacher preparation is to articulate and teach to standards of accomplished practice that incorporate the necessary understandings for successful work in urban communities.

PRINCIPLE THREE

Community teachers are developed through a system of practice-oriented, community-dedicated, and urban-focused instruction and assistance based in rich field experiences. The key to the system of practice that prepares community teachers is the immersion of candidates in rich contexts of collaborative activity and inquiry. This means several field experiences in a variety of urban community settings. These field experiences provide multiple opportunities to acquire and apply the range of situated knowledge and formal knowledge required for successful practice.

PRINCIPLE FOUR

Given sufficient opportunity to incorporate new understandings in systematic activity and the guided assistance of more skilled urban practitioners, any candidate can become a community teacher. Unquestionably, candidates of color bring knowledge and experiences to teacher preparation programs that are extremely valuable not only to their own future practice in urban schools but also to their classmates in schools of education. These may include, for example, fluency in a language other than English, familiarity with the nonverbal behaviors and other interactional patterns of urban students, firsthand knowledge of and experience in overcoming the kinds of obstacles faced by students growing up in poverty, shared commitment to the cultural values and perspectives of the nonmainstream community, the ability to motivate urban students, and facility in working collaboratively with others. These are very important strengths. Nonetheless, my experience as a teacher educator in an urban context has convinced me that, given appropriate motivation and educational experiences, European American candidates can achieve the same levels of accomplished practice as candidates of color.

PRINCIPLE FIVE

Developing the practice of community teachers requires a progressively leveled system for assisting the professional activity and performance of the candidate, where the assistance is provided by a collaborative network of colleagues rather than a single mentor teacher. The most significant forms of assistance come not from the apprenticeship-like relationship of a candidate to a mentor teacher. Rather, the appropriate assistance comes through the deliberate organization of systems of activity and collaborative work that surround the candidate and elevate his or her performance by supporting the day-to-day development of his or her teaching.

PRINCIPLE SIX

Preparing the accomplished teacher requires the "right" context of professional activity and development. For the *community teacher* framework provided in these pages, the "right" context consists of a systematically arranged circle of practitioners. This is a community-dedicated, urban-focused, practice-oriented field placement in which there is collaborative interaction among a network of professionals who are dedicated to the collateral work of educating children and preparing good teachers. Successful assistance of teaching performance requires a rich context of mutual development, conjoint purposeful activity in the advancement of teaching practice and learning achievement, collaboration, and critical inquiry into practice.

PRINCIPLE SEVEN

The contexts for advancing teaching practice need to be understood at multiple levels of expertise, experience, and activity, and as an ecology of practice within professional work. The key here is to use our understanding of levels of activity to enrich the systems of practice already in existence. For example, the clinical triad including a student teacher, cooperating teacher, and university supervisor should be extended to become a broader circle of practice that incorporates others who can assist both the student teacher's development and the general teaching practices in the classroom and the school.

SIGNIFICANCE OF CASE STUDIES

Clearly there are many dimensions to the crisis of knowledge facing teacher education. It is not that the community of educators is unaware of these issues. Rather, the threat to real progress is the inability to find the intellectual footing needed to grapple with all these issues at the same time. For this reason case studies of practice are used here. Each case study presented is designed to instruct practice. In particular, all are designed to illustrate the systems of practice that an urban-focused, community-dedicated, and practice-oriented school of education needs to produce community teachers.

All the practices illustrated in the cases are authentic. The events described are composites of actual settings, events, and episodes that I have observed or participated in as a teacher educator in an urban context. The case studies illustrate the developmental trajectory of the mostly European American, culturally mainstream, monolingual students with whom I work.

OVERVIEW OF BOOK

The book begins with an analysis of the dimensions of the new national agenda to improve the quality of teachers and teaching as a profession. Chapter 1 is an overview and analysis of the rapidly changing landscape, including recent government policy on both the federal and state levels, the responses of accrediting agencies and professional organizations, and the array of demands from public and private sectors to improve the quality of teaching. Case One in this chapter illustrates the nature of a crisis of knowledge and the dearth of concrete programs for implementing the new national agenda. Then it articulates necessary changes in our approach to teacher preparation if we are to meet the demand of providing competent, caring teachers for all the nation's children.

Chapter 2 introduces the *community teacher* framework for teacher training and development outlined in the seven principles presented earlier. The chapter identifies the special challenges of teacher education in light of the new national agenda focused on professionalizing teaching and elevating teaching quality as the main vehicles of school reform. The framework develops several key concepts, including the notions of the *community teacher, accomplished practice, circle of practice*, and *knowledge-in-practice*.

Chapter 3 continues the development of the theoretical framework, focusing on the notion of the *community teacher* as the ideal of accomplished practice for quality teaching and learning in culturally, linguistically, and economically diverse urban schools and communities. Using the major points of the new national agenda for the professionalization of teachers and the elevation of teacher quality, the chapter illustrates how urban teacher preparation can be synchronized with the national agenda. Case Two illustrates the first phase in the program experience of a community teacher.

Chapter 4 articulates how the ideas of the *community of practice* (Lave, 1988; Lave &Wenger, 1991) and *circle of practice* (Murrell, 1998) inform the development of urban teachers. Using Case Three to analyze contexts of practice communities, the chapter develops the notion of the community of practice, showing how a university moves from merely being a bilateral partner with a school to actively organizing a community of schools, higher-education partners, community stakeholders, funding agencies, and neighborhood constituencies. It examines the adaptation of the Professional Development Schools idea to work in urban schools and communities.

Chapter 5 outlines the developmental tasks of candidates learning to become teachers in light of the constraints, demands, and requirements of successful practice for the new millennium. It articulates what the architecture of professional knowledge for the successful, effective teacher looks like. It also provides an illustration of a program of study and conceptual framework. Case Four illustrates the transformation from the traditional clinical triad mode of student teaching to a circle of practice.

Chapter 6 formulates the contexts in which the assistance of teachers and candidates can take place to elevate their culturally competent practice in diverse urban schools. This chapter, through Case Five, articulates how we need to think about culture as it applies to the education of African American youngsters and other children of color. It explores the importance of multicultural competence and what it looks like for the community teacher.

Chapter 7 examines systems for improving instructional practice. The effectiveness of a teacher can be elevated through assistance to his or her practices as a teacher. This implies the assessment of performance—but for the purpose of improving the quality of teaching and learning activity, not to exclude or punish teachers. This chapter develops the notion of professionally assisted performance and articulates the systems of developing teachers' ability to develop and run high-quality instructional activity settings. This requires an urban-focused and community-responsive dimension of professional teacher knowledge that has received insufficient attention in the new articulations about the professional teacher nationwide. With Case Six, the chapter illustrates a sample university–community–school partnership and suggests ways that it might organize professional activity settings for improving teaching.

Chapter 8 addresses the role of research and researchers in the university–community–school partnerships.

Chapter 9 analyzes the new approaches of evaluating teacher quality, including the performance assessment approaches of the National Board for Professional and Teaching Standards (NBPTS) and the Interstate New Teacher Assessment and Support Consortium (INTASC). These are discussed in light of urban teaching and professional development schools.

On a final note, let me say that the presentation of the community teacher framework in these pages is, more or less, a composition of my professional life as a community teacher and urban educator. However, the fact that I have constructed the case descriptions from our work at Northeastern University in Boston should in no way be taken as an assertion that we have all the answers or have solved all the problems of reforming urban teaching and urban teaching reform. Neither should it be taken to mean that we are satisfied with our (still emerging) program for producing community teachers and accomplished urban educators. I hope that the honesty and authenticity in the characterizations of real events and real practice will result in a richer inquiry for the wider community of teacher educators.

Can we prepare successful, competent, and accomplished urban teachers to renew urban education? Indeed we can. It is a matter of developing what we know into a working system of practice, inquiry, and collaboration. This book brings such a system to life and, just as important, to *practice*.

CHAPTER 1

A Crisis of Knowledge-in-Practice in the Age of Teacher Education Reform

Above all else, we must resist attempts to reduce teacher education reform to one or two factors. For example, we must recognize that the "problem" of reform has political and institutional roots, not just intellectual and conceptual ones.
—*A. R. Tom*, Redesigning Teacher Education

THE WAY WE PREPARE TEACHERS and other school-based professionals is on the verge of radical transformation—as well it must be. Within the next 20 years, more than half the current teaching force will be leaving the profession, making drastic changes in professional development and teacher preparation inescapable. The nation's public schools will have to hire 2.5 million teachers over the next decade, about the same as the number of teachers now working (2.8 million). Just as dramatic as the shortage of teachers are the demographics of teachers and learners: Student populations are increasingly culturally diverse and non-White, and the population of teachers is increasingly monocultural and White.

In the last decade or so, improving the quality and professionalism of teachers has become the engine of school reform. Reports such as *What Matters Most* (National Commission on Teaching and America's Future [NCTAF], 1996) and *Building a Profession* (American Federation of Teachers [AFT], 2000) detail a number of factors that are instrumental in this change. Alarmingly, very little of what is being written and said addresses the demands of our increasingly diverse urban public schools. There is a dearth of historically and culturally situated inquiries on the requirements of quality learning and teaching, particularly where the demand and urgency are greatest—among diverse learners in urban public schools.

CRISIS IN URBAN EDUCATION AND URBAN COMMUNITIES

As stated earlier, education for children and youth in our nation's urban schools and communities is in a continuing state of crisis, and children of color are bearing the brunt. Schools, particularly in large metropolitan public systems, are failing Black and Latino children in epidemic proportions. Nationwide, Black and Latino students, who constitute the majority of students in virtually every urban school system, are disproportionately expelled, suspended, and relegated to special education programs in urban public schools. Fewer than 10% of African American and Latino men go to college. They constitute 76% of the nation's prison population. More Black and Latino young people drop out of high school than graduate, with dropout rates approaching two-thirds in many urban school systems. As of this writing, the number of African Americans going to college is actually declining. The longer Black children, particularly males, remain in school, the more their enthusiasm for learning and educational achievement diminishes (Comer & Poussaint, 1992; Kunjufu, 1983/1996).

Public education, long held out as America's hope of reversing poverty and powerlessness, simply does not work for the majority of youth in our nation's inner cities. The hope diminishes daily as standards-driven educational policies pave the way for greater privatization of public education and the erosion of a public trust in education. Added to this is the fact that segregated schooling has been on the rise since the late 1980s, with serious educational consequences.

There are two important ways in which this failure is being ignored by the national agendas for school reform. One is the formulation of, and fixation on, the *achievement gap,* a concept that focuses only on the disparities between White and non-White populations of students on the basis of their aggregate standardized test performance results. When performance disparities between populations of students are only recognized and dealt with in aggregate form, the policy solutions can never be specific enough to actually improve the learning experiences of the children of color who make up the bulk of the public school population. In virtually every case in which a district reports an initiative to "combat the achievement gap," the initiative is some form of merely promoting higher standards (Council of Great City Schools, 1999).

The second failure is the failure to disentangle poverty from race as an explanation of underachievement and deal with the actual social, economic, and political contexts of schooling for urban children. Black students, Hispanic students, and other students of color do not do less well in school *because* they are Black and Hispanic, but because an unacceptably high proportion of them go to impoverished schools. Impoverished schools do not produce the acceptable levels of achievement, engagement, and development. State, national, and international data typically show that high-poverty schools usually have lower levels of educational attainment than the national average. Orfield, Bachmeier, James, and Eitle (1997) detail some of the reasons why:

- High-poverty schools tend to draw less qualified teachers and hold them for shorter periods of time.
- High-poverty schools tend to invest more heavily in remediation at the cost of investment in the quality of the overall school program.
- Peer-group support and initiative building are lower in high-poverty schools.
- The general public generally holds high-poverty schools in lower esteem, as do parents who have no choice but to send their children to them.

REQUIRING MORE THAN MULTICULTURAL COMPETENCE

Clearly, the challenges to successful urban teaching are not simply a matter of working more effectively with children of color; a critical understanding is needed of how to effect change in the broader social, political, and historical context in which unequal schooling is constructed. It is quite true that the preparedness of preservice teachers critically depends on their ability to connect with learners from culturally, linguistically, and racially diverse communities. But the question is not so much how preservice teachers overcome their cultural encapsulation with respect to African American and Latino students. The real question is how to prepare students to understand and develop successful practice within the complexity of urban schools and communities in an era in which racism and poverty still fuel educational inequality.

The relationship across the nation between segregation by poverty and segregation by race in public schools is extremely close. By one measure (the proportion of students receiving free lunches), the correlation of high-poverty schools with high enrollments of African American and Latino students nationwide is .72 (Orfield et al., 1997). This indicates that racially segregated schools are highly likely to be segregated by poverty as well.

According to Orfield and colleagues (1997), only 1 out of 20 of the segregated schools in White communities face conditions of concentrated poverty, but 8 out of 10 segregated schools in Black and Latino communities face those conditions. This means that Black or Latino children who leave a segregated school setting for an integrated one are, on average, likely to improve their life chances. But recent Supreme Court rulings have given the green light for many metropolitan urban school districts to return to segregated schooling, making this kind of opportunity less likely in the future. The trends suggest a rapidly increasing racial isolation and geographic polarization.

These realities should be the foundation of the educational reform movements and the national agenda on improving the quality of teaching. These challenges to urban education should also be the foundation of urban teacher preparation. In spite of the new agenda for reforming schools through elevating teaching quality and the profession, teacher preparation still largely proceeds as if 23 of the 25 major city school systems were not comprised of a majority of people of color, principally Black and Latino, concentrated in poverty.

STANDARDS WITHOUT UNDERSTANDING ARE A MISTAKE

Not much can be done about improving teaching and learning in America without addressing the social and historical contexts of urban school systems and the structural inequality in education that emanates from these contexts. Yet all the attention seems directed at creating policy regarding how to professionalize teaching and standardize assessment and accountability systems. This is not to say that the agenda to improve the quality of teaching is unimportant, but rather that the agenda is shortsighted and limited if it is not placed in broader cultural, historical, and political contexts and if the real and tangible needs of diverse populations of urban students are not acknowledged. Before we create standards of quality, we must know *well* what quality *means* in those arenas where quality education is most needed.

Do we want to standardize aspects of the profession before we have a handle on *accomplished practice* (or at least *competent practice*) for the areas of greatest educational need? Do we want to set as "standards of practice" contemporary approaches that have thus far proven unequal to the task of promoting quality education for all children? As for the policy making on accountability, should we not first determine the *nature* of accomplished practice before holding practitioners *accountable* to standards of practice? Should we support "standards-based reform" at all if there is no dedication to developing accomplished practice where it is most needed—namely, urban schools?

These are questions too few are asking in the national frenzy to "raise the bar" for teachers without asking whether doing so actually improves the pool of accomplished teachers. Consider the following facts:

- In at least 38 states, departments of education or legislative action require some form of teacher test as a condition of licensure.
- In at least 36 states, a written assessment (not an assessment of actual teaching performance) is required for new teachers.
- Although 36 states have special programs to recruit "minority" teachers, the proportion of teachers of color is decreasing in relation to the proportion of students of color.
- Virtually all teacher tests have unacceptably high "adverse impacts data" (data comparing "minority" to "nonminority" candidates) results: The percentage of test failure is disproportionately high among candidates of color.

But in the current policy-making flurry to "raise the bar" for entering the teaching profession, the litany of school failure continues for the nation's Black and Latino students, as well as other students of color.

HOW DO WE GET ACCOMPLISHED
PRACTICE IN URBAN SCHOOLS?

Clearly, there are structural inequalities that limit access to quality education for children of color in underresourced urban communities. But there are knowable aspects of accomplished practice that are being ignored in the rhetoric of the national agenda to improve teachers and teaching. We should be far more concerned about what accomplished practice will mean in the context of public education's biggest failures and demand that specifics be added to the call for "caring, competent teachers in every classroom" in the NCTAF report and similar publications.

As a national community of educators, we can agree that the quality of teachers' practice is the single most critical factor in elevating the quality of student learning (NCTAF, 1996). What we have not agreed on is what quality teaching (accomplished practice) looks like among African

American and Latino learners in urban school districts. We do not agree on how to put people in the position of becoming an accomplished teacher. In the absence of such agreement, a rush to teacher testing is the wrong national priority.

What we need, as a national community of educators, is a "performance perspective" to replace the ubiquitous "gatekeeping perspective" prevalent in standards-based reform and high-stakes testing. Analogous to Tharp and Gallimore's (1991) perspective on *performance* (see also Wiggins & McTighe, 1998; Wiske, 1998) is the idea that we train and develop teachers by assisting them in the practices of teaching. Just as we would want to account for student learning in an *understanding performance* (where they do thoughtful things with the content they learn), we should want to account for the accomplished practice of quality teachers in terms of *accomplished performance*.

No focus is more important than the *actual and demonstrated ability* of teachers and the educational professionals who work in urban schools. Unfortunately, there is little on the horizon that offers hope of preparing teachers for accomplished practice in the areas of greatest need—urban public schools. The serious challenge for teacher preparation is how to develop practice and create the conditions to promote accomplished performance of candidates, while at the same time eliminating the structural inequalities in institutions and society.

NATIONAL IMPETUS TOWARD PERFORMANCE-BASED ASSESSMENT

In 1996 the NCTAF issued a report concluding that the teaching profession had been degraded over the years by uneven teacher education, hit-or-miss induction of new teachers, and outdated systems for evaluating, rewarding, and developing teaching practice. To address this, Congress passed the Higher Education Act of 1998. Title II of that legislation calls for reforms in the training of teachers and teaching quality. In addition to providing competitive grants for the improvement of teaching quality through the formation of partnerships between local schools and universities, it has imposed a new reporting and accountability system. According to this system, every state must establish a uniform reporting system of the performance of every teacher education program in the state and issue state "report cards" for teacher preparation institutions.

In spite of the new national commitment to improve teacher quality with an emphasis on work in high-need urban schools and communities, teacher preparation has yet to show any greater capacity to prepare teachers for successful work in diverse urban school settings (Darling-Hammond, 1994; Melnick & Zeichner, 1997; NCTAF, 1996; Murrell, 1991, 1997, 1998; Zeichner, 1996). National initiatives purportedly targeted at improving equity and effective teaching in diverse contexts (e.g., Title II of the Education Act of 1998, professional development schools (PDSs), the federal government's Goals 2000 initiative, the Holmes Group) have not yet yielded any indications of (1) improved educational outcomes for African American children and other children of color or (2) increases in the number of teachers able to work effectively with African American children (cf. Comer, 1997; Irvine & Fraser, 1998; Labaree & Pallas, 1996; Murrell, 1998; Myers, 1996b; Sykes, 1997; Valli, Cooper, & Frankes, 1997; Vavrus, 1995).

There are no articulations of accomplished practice in the recent NCTAF program, the recent Title II higher education amendments, or the Holmes Partnership proposals (Holmes Group, 1986, 1990) that would lead us to expect the next generation of teachers to be any more successful in diverse urban environments than they have been in the past decade, despite PDS and other reform initiatives (see, e.g., Andrew, 1997, Murrell, 1998, Valli et al., 1997; Vavrus, 1995; Zeichner, 1996).

The best we have is a set of national, regional, and local imperatives to develop the profession in new ways that address the critical failure of schooling in diverse urban communities. But there are missing pieces, most notably the issues of education in culturally, linguistically, and economically diverse urban communities. For example, it is highly significant that the efforts to develop professional teaching standards (such as the work of the National Board for Professional Teaching Standards [NBPTS] and the Interstate New Teacher Assessment and Support Consortium [INTASC]) have not incorporated work on culturally responsive pedagogy in any meaningful way that relates to quality teaching and learning in diverse urban contexts (Irvine & Fraser, 1998).

It is my contention that, although many aspects of the current reform efforts have been proposed to improve the quality of teachers, the prospects of improving teaching and learning will likely worsen where improvements are most needed—in underresourced urban public schools. The reason is that there is a crisis of knowledge—a glaring absence of a systematic, coherent framework for organizing partnership work in university–school collaborations. The reasons for this lack of coherence are many, but they can be summarized as a disconnection from practice. Policy is set, standards are mandated, and curricula are designed independently of practice and the understanding of the lived experiences of learners and teachers in the day-by-day activities of learning and teaching.

CRISIS OF KNOWLEDGE WORSENS TEACHER QUALITY

Initiatives for school reform that lack a commitment to developing accomplished practice actually stand to worsen prospects of success because energies are not focused on pedagogy—on promoting quality teaching and learning. *Performance assessment* and *professionalization* of teachers are at the center of the national and regional agendas to ensure caring and competent teachers for every classroom (NCTAF, 1996). Lacking in the national agenda for improving teacher quality is the commitment to developing accomplished practice, and a commitment to "learning in practice."

To improve the quality of teaching and learning, SCDEs (schools, colleges, and departments of education) leadership will have to reprioritize the agenda, so that the development of practice is pushed to the forefront to address the inability of public schools and school systems in America to successfully educate the children who inhabit America's underside.

Up to now, the SCDE community has taken too seriously the agenda to improve professional standards and taken too lightly the means for developing accomplished practice. Without an agenda for articulating and developing an accomplished practice, the national agenda has no chance of increasing educational success among African American children and other children of color in urban communities.

What must happen in the reorganization of educational leadership in the SCDE community to enable it to take on the real tasks of improving teaching in diverse urban contexts? Simply put: a greater focus on practice, a greater humility in working in collaboration with parents and communities, and a disposition toward inquiry-in-practice. To exhibit the necessary leadership for change, the SCDE community must first reject the fallacious assumption that simply "raising the bar" (in order to get "better" teachers) will improve teaching and learning in urban public schooling. The new leadership must also recognize that the crisis in urban schools in underresourced communities requires a more sophisticated response than that of simply "tooling up teachers." This is especially true given the dearth of knowledge about accomplished practice in urban settings. The "right tools" are not really available.

WHAT'S MISSING IN THE AGENDA TO
IMPROVE TEACHING QUALITY?

Critics of school reform rarely examine this disconnect, this lack of balance and bad ecology of policy and practice. What is missing is a logical, coherent, effective system of professional development and a working conception of how collaborative partnerships can promote the quality of teaching while also improving accomplished practice. There is a sizable educational reform literature that laments the limitations of contemporary approaches to professional development. Four of these laments are important to this discussion (Darling-Hammond & Sykes, 1999). First is the issue of *fragmented delivery*, meaning that professional development is too often offered as a one-shot workshop focused on a limited topic or array of ideas. The most teacher participants can hope for in this situation is to get one or two new ideas or activities they can appropriate for their classroom.

A second issue is the limited way in which the professional development of practicing teachers has been construed. Historically, professional development has seldom been viewed as a cohesive and continuous development toward accomplished levels of practice. Most often, professional development is viewed as a certification of "seat time" or a credentialing of professional activity. Third, professional development as it is currently offered carries few expectations that the participation of teachers will yield any demonstrable elevation of their teaching practice. Finally, there is rarely an infrastructure to support professional development that links the professional inquiry of teachers to their work in, or the needs of, the school context. In short, what is missing with regard to professional development is the *means to an aim*—activity that requires teachers to become serious students of their own practice.

What is also missing in the broader context of the policy arena is an articulation of the *aims for quality teaching*—particularly for the populations and locations that are in the most serious need of quality teaching and learning. In reality, the educational policy makers are in the worst position to make decisions about teaching practice. There is a mean irony to a situation in which policy makers call for "making teaching more of a profession" on one hand, and then make policy decisions that utterly diminish teachers' professional responsibility on the other hand (Hargreaves, 1994). Policy decisions are made about practices, activities, and struggles about which the policy makers have little informed, practice-based, or firsthand knowledge. The people engaged daily in the practices of teaching and learning ought to be the first ones asked about what makes sense in order to elevate the quality of teaching and learning. Instead, the tendency is for the people furthest removed from schools and classrooms to set policy and the agenda for improving the quality of teaching.

Finally, it is interesting to note in almost every policy proposal on improving the quality of teaching the lack of recognition of divergent political and ideological perspectives. From the perspective of a grassroots practitioner, particularly one of color, the arrogance is quite remarkable.

An African American colleague of mine, whose educational practice is firmly rooted in the urban community, has coined a term to describe the constellation of well-intentioned, too-far-removed policy makers. She calls them the "great White school reformers." In her view, the current crisis of knowledge in urban education stems from the failure to draw on the local knowledge, perspectives, and cultural frameworks of people of color in diverse urban communities. Her view is that without being a participant in the doings of the community surrounding education and teachers, one can rarely develop a real understanding of what is going on and what people believe, value, and want accomplished. While this view is shared by many teachers of color, it is rarely taken with sufficient seriousness by professional educators and policy makers.

THE CRISIS OF KNOWLEDGE
AS A PROBLEM OF POLITICS

As discussed earlier, policy makers who talk and write about the issues and problems of urban education lack real access to the immediacy of practice. The result of this is that ideological issues and conflict are not adequately addressed. As an African American scholar and educator who has spent his adult life examining the prospects of quality education for African American children, I have little faith that the contemporary educational reform coming in the form of policy will in any way reverse the long-standing educational inequality for African Americans and other historically marginalized groups.

The ideologies of current educational thinkers and policy makers virtually guarantee the continuation of structured inequality. The dominant ideology of American schooling is imbued with cultural values inimical to the historical legacy of African American educational and cultural values. One of these is the value of rugged individualism that distorts and hides the ugly construction of disadvantage in school practices. Another is the belief in competition as the appropriate means of organizing social relations and human systems in schools.

It is the American system of ideas and values embodied as a dominant ideology—tacitly assumed and uncritically accepted by teachers and practitioners—that perpetuates the system of structured inequality. This is one area in which university participation should be able to make a huge contribution to the elevation of urban teaching practice. The community of professionals in teacher preparation can never be on the leading edge of the responsive reshaping of their work as long as they fail to define their aims in terms of the most serious shortcomings in practice. And by practice I mean both professional activity and the use of theory emanating from professional knowledge that contests social inequality, racism, and modern forms of oppression. Let me try to illustrate these concerns in the following case study.

CASE ONE

Imagine that the following description is about school–university partnership that, by all criteria of the professional organizations that advocate the PDS model, is the "model PDS."

The school partner is the new Martin Luther King Pilot School, a K–5 elementary school located in a large metropolitan school district in New England. Formerly known as the Quincy Adams, the school was restructured this fall and is destined to become a K–8 school as it adds a sixth, seventh, and eighth grade in each of the next 3 years in accordance with its recently approved charter as a pilot school. The school is located in an underresourced neighborhood in the city and is a 5-minute walk from the campus of the partnering university in the PDS relationship. More than half of the school's students come from a nearby public housing project, and more than 70% are on a subsidized or free lunch program. The composition almost exactly mirrors the ethnic percentages of the entire school district. For the previous 3 years, the school population had averaged 49% Black, 26% Latino, 15% White, and 10% other. However, when it opened this past fall, the enrollments for both Black and White students dramatically increased, resulting in a 68% Black and 20% White enrollment, along with an Latino enrollment of 12%.

The university partner is a major research university with a sizable school of education and a mission to work specifically in urban schools. The school of education has initiated a number of informal partnership relationships with the neighborhood schools involving student teacher and intern placements and a number of formal PDS types of partnerships. The King Pilot School is one of those PDS partnerships. However, two of the education faculty involved in the partnership—Ms. Kay, the field coordinator, and Mr. Zed, an assistant professor of curriculum and instruction— had been active in the school over the last 5 years. Both of them are White, and both were instrumental in transforming the long-standing informal relationship between the school and the university into a true PDS relationship with more formal arrangements and agreements. The opportunity to create the PDS arrangement occurred early in the previous spring semester through the confluence of several events. The retirement of the school's principal paved the way for the school department's approval of a petition submitted by a group of parents and community activists for the Quincy Adams school to become the Martin Luther King Pilot School. So-called pilot schools are public schools granted special status by the administration when the school community has its proposal for an innovative restructuring of school mission, curricula, and instructional delivery approved. The status permits the school greater flexibility in decision making, hiring of school personnel, and organizational design than is the case for other public schools—analogous to the charter school idea. Following approval of the petition, a steering committee was formed to put the charter (framework and plan of operation) of the new pilot school into action.

Insiders of the central administration revealed to the school's steering committee that a significant factor in approving the petition to become a pilot school was the potential that the school would enter into a PDS relationship with the university. The mission of the chartering document specifies a whole-school focus on science and mathematics, with specific attention to meeting the needs of African American and Latino students.

The new pilot school had a number of complex problems to confront. Morale at the school was low, and there was friction between two major factions in the faculty. On one hand were a group of young White teachers who described themselves as "progressive," most of whom had been teaching for less than 5 years. On the other side of an ideological divide was a cadre of older Black teachers, most of whom had been with the school since it opened as the Quincy Adams School in 1976. As "discipline problems" seemed to worsen and student performance seemed to drop throughout the 1980s and into the 1990s, the faculty became polarized between Black and White teachers who began to blame each other for the school's worsening reputation.

The group of White progressive teachers complained that the Black principal was too autocratic, authoritarian, arbitrary, and "out of touch with the new ideas." For her part, the former principal had always been able to maintain group civility and keep the warring factions under wraps. In heated faculty meetings, for example, she would make people listen respectfully to one another and would not let people get out of hand. Overall, the former principal had done a good job of holding the community of teachers together. But with the principal's retirement and the transformation of the Quincy Adams into the Martin Luther King Pilot School, the warring factions came to new life.

One of the most divisive issues had to do with the overwhelmingly White presence on the steering committee that was making decisions about the school. At the end of the schoolyear and following the principal's retirement party, a number of the progressive White teachers and a handful of White parents had gotten together to develop the charter proposal for the school to become a pilot school, a document that had to be submitted at the central office before the beginning of the fall semester. None of the Black faculty members had been informed about this meeting.

Mr. Zed and Ms. Kay from the university had attended these three meetings and participated in the drafting of the charter. Evidently, neither of them had raised concerns about the fact that no people of color were participants in the meetings. This meeting group of about 20 White parents, 10 progressive White teachers, and the 2 representatives from the university had begun calling itself the Leadership Committee. After receiving preliminary approval of the charter document on August 1, the school had officially became a pilot school. At that point the group called itself the Leadership Committee of the Martin Luther King Pilot School. The committee's first order of business had been to appoint a search committee to hire a new principal, who had not been automatically replaced because of the pending change to a pilot school.

Curiously, the advertising for the position had not appeared in any of the usual publications—local, regional, or national. Members of the Leadership Committee had approached several potential principals. Within a 2-week time frame, the Leadership Committee had hired a principal— Ms. Payne, a dynamic, vocal woman who was reputed to be a sort of "hotshot" educational reformer. She was a White career educator in her early forties who had published a great deal on progressive education and had successfully started a school in another city that since had become a "national model." To accept the principalship, she left her job in an independent organization doing work on parental involvement and the development of urban schools. The Black faculty, unaware of the Leadership Committee's meetings during the summer, was stunned to discover that a new principal, whom they had never met, had been hired in mid-August.

PDS ORGANIZATIONAL MEETING

When the new principal arrived, the White parents and White teachers viewed her arrival as their opportunity to "get the school in shape." In mid-August, the Leadership Committee and the new principal called a PDS organizational meeting. The meeting had been advertised as an all-school organizational meeting called by the parents council, a group dominated by young and liberal White parents. The only official, formal advertisement of the meeting had been a one-page flyer that went out as a parent mailing.

At the first organizational meeting of the PDS, all 10 of the young progressive teachers were there, as well as the principal, the field coordinator, and several members of the parents council. However, none of the

Black teachers or any Black or Latino parents were present. When one of the White teachers, Ms. Hall, expressed concern about the lack of Black and Latino representation at the meeting, a colleague angrily retorted: "All the teachers knew about the meeting, so they could have come if they wanted to; and we sent a notice home to all the parents in English *and* Spanish, so they could have come, too, if they were interested."

The agenda for the meeting was to finalize the PDS agreements and select the participating teachers who would have student teaching interns from the university. As the discussion about selection criteria for intern placements continued, Ms. Hall, essentially silent throughout, became increasingly uncomfortable. So far in the discussion, not a single Black teacher's name had been proposed as a possible candidate to receive an intern. Gulping hard, Ms. Hall entered the conversation. "What about Mrs. Jones?" she suggested, naming one of the most senior and best-loved members of the Black faculty. "I think she'd make a great mentor for interns." An uncomfortable silence ensued. Finally one of the teachers said:

> Yes, Mrs. Jones is a wonderful person, but I can't agree with a lot of the stuff she does in the classroom. She's too rigid. She doesn't let the children express their own views or do anything interesting or creative. Everything is by the book, follow the rules. That isn't going to work with an intern. The interns will be bringing in all these new ideas from their professors, and Mrs. Jones will be like, "No, I don't think that's going to work here, honey." If we're going to change this school, we need new ideas; we need to try creative things. Mrs. Jones is nice and all that, but she's not going to add to that.

The other teachers nodded in agreement. Although she did not really agree with her colleagues' assessment, Ms. Hall did not know how to respond, how to put her objections into words. It was true that Mrs. Jones was formal in her approach and strict with the children, but her students loved her and they seemed to be learning—not that she had any real evidence about that, of course. And then it *was* true that Mrs. Jones rarely seemed to express much enthusiasm when people came up with new ideas at the curriculum meetings. Maybe she *was* kind of rigid. In the end, Ms. Hall said nothing to defend Mrs. Jones. Instead, she suggested another Black teacher, Adeena Britt, a younger kindergarten teacher who seemed to be extremely popular with children's families.

One of the teachers quickly responded by shaking her head vigorously and then saying:

No, no, that won't work, and it is not just because I personally don't agree with her teaching style, which I don't. I do think there's a range of good teaching styles. But with some things, you have to draw the line because you have to go by what the research says. I just took a course at your university (*nodding toward Mr. Zed*) called "The Meaning and Development of Play," and it was a great course. The professor was talking about how children really need to play. She said that an amazing amount of development occurs through play. After hearing that and looking at all the research supporting it, now it makes me feel even worse when I walk past Adeena's room and see her kids hunched over working on their letters when they should be playing. I don't think Adeena realizes how much happier her children would be, and how much more they would really be learning, if she would just let the activities emerge from the children. So what if they want to spend an extra 10 minutes in the block area? As long as they're engaged and interacting, they're learning! I'm not talking against Adeena. I think she is great and all and some of the parents really like her, but she's not the right person for this intern program.

As Ms. Hall got ready to respond, she was quickly cut off by another colleague, who said impatiently, her remarks clearly directed at Ms. Hall, "This isn't about race. It is about doing what's best for children, *especially* the children of color." Ms. Hall did not respond.

As they sat listening to the discussion, both Ms. Kay, the field coordinator, and Mr. Zed, the liaison, noticed the high frequency of remarks from teachers containing a rhetoric of multiculturalism. The teachers often remarked, for instance, about their "commitment to diversity," recounting several times how they had come to select the new name—the Martin Luther King, Jr., Pilot School—and how this name symbolized their commitments to social justice and communities of color. However, as Ms. Kay and Mr. Zed both observed, again and again in the conversation, these commitments seemed belied by the disparaging remarks made about Black teachers. Despite their awareness of this contradiction and their concern about it, neither Ms. Kay nor Mr. Zed brought it up for discussion. After all, they were not in the school on a daily basis. They weren't really that familiar with the Black teachers' classrooms. Perhaps there *were* major problems in those rooms. And, as one teacher had pointed out, Black faculty could have attended this meeting. They knew about it, just as everyone else did.

Not surprisingly, by the end of the meeting, all of the interns had been assigned to White teachers in the school, including Ms. Hall. These assignments would provide teachers not only with opportunities to learn from and mentor a novice teacher, but also with a number of other benefits provided by the PDS arrangement, including release time for professional development, vouchers to take courses at the university, and university privileges (use of the library, recreation center, etc.). Clearly the stage was set for conflict.

PRECIPITATING CONFLICT

At a faculty meeting in November, Ms. Hall announced that at the pre-Thanksgiving assembly her third-grade students would be presenting their final projects from the unit on American slavery that had served as the focus point of her intern's curriculum unit. After making this announcement, she observed a Black faculty member saying something to the other Black teachers sitting near her, after which they all laughed. Ms. Hall had the feeling that these teachers were being critical or making fun of her in some way, and she resented it. What reason did they have to be critical when she and her student intern were working so hard to teach the children in her classroom about African American history? Why couldn't the Black teachers appreciate that effort or at least respect it? After all, she was on their side, and she had worked hard to ensure that her student intern was as well.

During the morning assembly Ms. Hall was visibly nervous, but she quickly began to relax as she watched her third-graders perform in front of family members and the school community. The children had put so much effort into their work, and their performances reflected it. The children's performances were based on their responses to two children's books about slavery, one a story about a young girl who escaped from slavery by following the clues embedded in the pattern of a patchwork quilt and the other a fictionalized account of Frederick Douglass's resistance to his slave master and his eventual escape to freedom. Based on the first book, the majority of Ms. Hall's class had decided to create their own freedom quilts, their colorful paper quilt squares attached together with purple yarn. Now, as the children displayed their quilts, each of them talked about his or her personal desire for freedom.

One child said that he wanted the freedom to choose his own videos when his family went to Blockbuster, another the freedom to pick out her own clothes, another the freedom to get a perm if she wanted to, another the freedom to play after school without his little brother tagging along. Ms. Hall smiled fondly as she listened, for at least the dozenth time, to her students describe their innocent and childlike notions of freedom. "They are so adorable," she thought to herself as the quilt group returned to their seats and the rest of her class started to perform the play they had written about Frederick Douglass's escape to freedom.

The play, based heavily on the children's book the class had read, portrayed Douglass as an exceptional and exemplary individual, articulate and outspoken, very different from his fellow slaves, who hung their heads and did as they were told. Unlike Douglass, these slaves lacked the courage to stand up to the cruel slave breaker, Covey. As Douglass took an imaginary swing at Covey, some of the children in the audience began to clap. This scattering of applause grew louder when Covey, who had been flung to the ground by Douglass's blow, stood up and said solemnly to Douglass: "I guess I underestimated you, Frederick. You may be a slave, but you are a very brave man."

At the end of the play, the young actors and actresses stood in a row as, one by one, they made declarations about what they might have done to strike a blow for freedom had they been slaves in the nineteenth century. When one boy said proudly that he would have picked up his shotgun and "blasted the slave owner good," some children started clapping again. Behind her, Ms. Hall heard Adeena Britt, the Black kindergarten teacher, let out a deep breath as she said quite loudly, "I absolutely cannot believe this!" Many of the African American parents in the audience were also visibly quite upset.

Ms. Britt was not the only person who was upset. Along with the entire Black faculty, the Black parents who had been in the audience were also furious. Without even needing to discuss the issue with one another, Black teachers and parents felt a collective sense of outrage over how the unspeakable horrors of slavery had been trivialized and distorted by the children's performances. That very afternoon, a group of 10 parents expressed their ire to the principal. Ms. Payne, the new principal, wasn't very successful in calming them down, but she did get them to agree to come to a "town meeting"—a new means of community talk and decision making that the school had yet to try out. She promised the parents, "We'll iron everything out then."

News of this event quickly spread throughout the school. The planned agenda for the faculty meeting for that afternoon was quickly thrown out as Black and White teachers exchanged heated comments with one another for almost the entire meeting. Ms. Payne was unable to bring the faculty to order. As faculty got up to leave at 4:30, one of the Black teachers told the liason, Mr. Zed (who regularly attended faculty meetings): "Now with Ms. Bethune [the principal who had just retired], none of this would have happened. Those teachers would not have dared to put on a shameful performance like that, and those parents would have been heard. They would not have been put off like that for some stupid town meeting that's going to be all about listening to what the White folks have to say, as usual!"

The town meeting that occurred the Monday after Thanksgiving break quickly turned into a shouting match polarized along racial lines. The White parents and teachers advocated for the importance of African American history being a part of the curriculum and for teachers having the academic freedom to try out new ideas, even if not all those ideas worked out perfectly the first time or met with everyone's approval. One White teacher said: "A school community is a democracy. In a democracy, people aren't all expected to think alike!" The Black teachers and parents argued back that it was disrespectful for White teachers in the school to design a curriculum on African American history without bothering to seek the advice and help of Black teachers in the school. "And what's more," shouted one Black teacher, "y'all do not know enough about our history to even get it right, let alone show any respect for it. The idea that you would have children standing up in front of an audience equating the freedom to pick out videos with enslaved Africans' dream of freedom just makes me sick to my stomach!" Many of the parents expressed the view that a line had been crossed when they had not been consulted, or even apprised of the fact, that the issue of slavery would come up in the lessons of their children.

Finally, Ms. Payne attempted to restore order and to make her support of academic freedom clear. She said passionately: "We have to have the academic freedom here to develop curriculum that is meaningful in children's lives and that reflects their cultural experience. I know that slavery is a difficult subject to discuss, but if we don't talk about it, how else are children going to learn about their roots?" There was a chorus of gasps among the Black teachers and parents at this remark. One Black mother said, "Oh, so now we're going to learn about our roots in slavery from the descendants of the people who enslaved us!" Now the chorus of gasps came from the White teachers in the room. Mr. Zed saw that the meeting was out of control, understanding that a lot more was fueling the anger of these parents. He stood up and said, "Look, we are trying to build a democratic community of practice here that includes everybody—where everyone's view is respected . . ." A parent nearby cut him off by saying aloud "We lost that respect when Ms. Bethune left." Mr. Zed continued by suggesting a mediation process to come to some kind of resolution. One parent, Mr. Douglas, complained bitterly: "You can go ahead and mediate all you want, but we know what the outcome is going to be. You just want us to participate in your little game to make it seem like we had some say in the matter.

Truth is, all of your minds are already made up. Tell me, why is it that all you folks have all the answers when you don't even know us?"

Then Mr. Douglas turned to Mr. Zed and Ms. Kay, who were sitting together, and asked, "And how you gonna come in here and tell us what we have to expose our children to? You say you support this?" When each nodded their heads, Mr. Douglas said firmly, "Well, if you got voted in, you can get voted out. We didn't ask you to be in this, so we're going to see that you get put out!" In the ensuing discussion, many of the parents made it plain that the decisions leading up to the school becoming a PDS did not include the majority of parents who were out in full force tonight. The meeting ended in chaos, and many of the parents, White and Black, milled out of the cafetorium in anger. Mr. Zed appealed to Mr. Douglas to get himself placed on the agenda of the "Let's take back our school!" meeting of parents being planned for the following Saturday at the youth center. After some heated discussion, Mr. Douglas reluctantly agreed, saying, "You know, we're extending you a courtesy you failed to extend to us in setting up this cozy little university partnership where you all do whatever you want to do."

THE MEANING OF PREPARING THE COMMUNITY TEACHER

The case is a composite of a dynamic that frequently occurs in school–university partnerships. I used it to illustrate the essential qualities of the theoretical framework of the community teacher and community partnerships for the renewal of urban schools. I now summarize nine qualities necessary for collaborative school–university partnerships to elevate the quality of urban schools without replicating the worst of their failures with African American, Latino, and other children of color.

1. A "QUALITY OF EDUCATION" PERSPECTIVE

The first essential quality is a conception of quality education formed from the perspective of the communities, students, and families being served. There is a strong heritage of education in the African American community that many of the parents in this case held regarding the schooling of their children (cf. Woodson, 1933/1990). The younger faculty, the principal, and the university faculty were largely unaware of this tradition, as is frequently the case in PDS partnerships. As a result, they devalued, degraded, and ultimately dismissed local and cultural knowledge that they really needed in order to have a chance of being effective educators with the children in front of them. As long as this continues, no amount of funding, resources, computers, books, or special programs will make any difference in Martin Luther King Pilot School's path toward destroying the minds and degrading the development of Black children.

Conceiving of "equity" in terms of practices that lead to quality education as desired by the parents would have meant respecting the parents' perspectives and desire to be heard regarding this concern. Instead, the predominant notion of equity in the school was one that translated to "multiculturalism" and "diversity," a frequent conflation of ideas made by otherwise progressive educators. But conflating issues of equity with issues of diversity failed to address what was really at stake—what it takes to elevate the achievement and development of the African American and Latino children in the school. The progressive teachers' pride in the trifling gesture of naming the school stood in stark contrast to their practices of exclusion and cultural hegemony in handling the issues of curriculum content with the African American community, as well as their nascent racism in carrying out these practices.

Without a circle of practice that includes membership of parents and stakeholders from the wider community, the school will not have the critical lens necessary for interrogating what "educational quality" and "equity" really mean to the people the school is supposed to serve. Critical interrogation of the concept of "educational equity" has been conspicuously absent in both the advocacy and research literature on PDSs and the policy literature advocating collaborative partnerships involving schools, universities, and communities. A community partnership approach to professional development shifts from an "equality of schooling," or everyone-gets-the-same perspective, to a "quality of teaching and learning" perspective. With such a shift, we would no longer perceive equity merely in terms of "racial balance" or equivalent numbers of books and computers, but primarily in terms of *effect*—whether children's experiences of the curriculum and scholastic achievement are actually improved.

2. A "COLLABORATIVE, MULTILATERAL PARTNERSHIP" PERSPECTIVE

The second quality is partnership formation that is open not only to community constituencies—parents and parent organizations, community agencies that work with the same children, and other stakeholders—but also to conjoint collaboration with other institutions and community-based agencies. On this account, the school people violated any sense of inclusion and democratic practice. They seem to have already decided an issue that was vitally important to the parents, as happens time and again in school–university partnerships that do not regard parents to be partners. Although the parents may not have been opposed to either the intern's practice or the instructional unit, the outcome that both trivialized and misrepresented the experience of African Americans was too much. The parents appreciated that interns are not going to be strong teachers, but they considered the failure to apprise them of the subject matter a major breech by the school administration. From the perspective of the parents, the insensitivity and the arrogance cascaded to a point that they could no longer tolerate. To be told that they would be able to discuss their concerns at a later meeting, only to find that the meeting was not at all set up to address such concerns was, justifiably, the last straw.

What is missing in the contemporary way in which school–university partnerships are formed is *humility of practice*. That is, schools of education in partnership with school faculty have to avoid the fatal assumption that they know all they need to know about the culture, values, traditions, and heritages of the people they purportedly serve. The need is to organize human systems in schools to elevate practice, which requires accessing knowledge from those who have it.

3. A "POSITIONALITY" PERSPECTIVE

Teachers' work is not simply a matter of acquiring the appropriate skills, techniques, and expertise but also includes being politically reflective and ideologically interpretive. As Cochran-Smith (1996) argues, the development of effective work in urban sites "is about interpretation, ideologies, and practices and the ways that these are interdependent with, and informed by, each other." She rightly argues that teachers' knowledge from this perspective is not simply about skills and techniques, or what people frequently refer to as "best practice."

The school people—the principal and the young faculty—were missing the humility of practice that would allow them to acknowledge that they have much to learn about, and with, the people they purportedly serve.

4. A COMMUNITY DEVELOPMENT AGENDA

Teacher preparation ought to be predicated on how to operate within the context of a community development *agenda*. One part of the African American tradition of education is the theme that education is for the development of the community. On one level this means acknowledging, learning about, and drawing upon the cultural resources of African Americans. On another level this means authentic engagement with the children in front of you as a teacher. Regardless of how well prepared teachers are, or how excellent the curriculum, children still cannot learn when they come to school hungry, angry, afraid, disaffected, unwell, or conflicted. The total contexts in which children grow, learn, and develop are necessary considerations in promoting their academic achievement and personal development. This idea is best exemplified in the Comer (1997) model.

A community partnership perspective would be helpful to guide the new school leadership in some of the ways of the departing community teacher—Ms. Bethune, who understood that schools are extensions of the community.

5. A "SCHOLAR–TEACHER" PERSPECTIVE

A fifth necessity is a focus on visioning and developing a new kind of teacher for effectively meeting the challenges of successful work in urban schools and communities in the 21st century. This would require teacher preparation focused on a new and different kind of teacher, one who recognizes, understands, and effectively negotiates complexities of urban communities that impact children's learning and development. This new and different kind of teacher would need to be assisted in professional contexts that honor collaboration, the humility of practice, and cultural/local knowledge of the people in the community. The Martin Luther King Pilot School had several community teachers—the accomplished African American teachers. The school neither recognized nor drew upon the expertise of its accomplished teachers.

6. A "RELATIONSHIPS OVER BUREAUCRACIES" PERSPECTIVE

A sixth necessity is a patently antibureaucratic mode of interaction among partners that permits flexibility of collaboration and involves all stakeholders in the enterprise of educating and developing children. This flexible collaboration is required in order to invite the participation of parents, community members, and all stakeholders necessary for effective problem definition and resolution.

The most important feature we would expect to find in an urban-focused, equity-minded, diversity-responsive, and inquiry-based PDS is attention to building democratic organizations in light of the social, cultural, and political realities of urban schools. Critical pedagogy is a perspective that encourages critical reflection about how we, as university people, enter into partnership with school communities. Critical pedagogy is a perspective that acknowledges that we do not fully know what to do and to think until we couple our doing and thinking with a process of joint public discourse and community building.

Consequently, our research, our theory, and our program development must be closely linked to the everyday practical activities of school and community development. This means the elimination of "helperism" in our relationship to our partners in urban communities and working with them on *their* enterprises of change. From this perspective, the broader purpose of higher education in the life of urban communities ought to be as a participant in transforming these communities, as the means of moving society toward becoming a truly just, multicultural democracy. Therefore, the primary work of an urban-focused, equity-minded partnership is building community on a multiplicity of levels—both inter- and intrainstitutional.

7. AN "EXPANDED ROLES" PERSPECTIVE

As stated earlier, a public, community-centered, and child-focused approach to building partnerships is essential to the project of developing an urban-focused, equity-minded, diversity-responsive, and inquiry-based professional relationship. Otherwise, perspectives that need to be surfaced, confronted, and negotiated will remain unvoiced. But within this partnership building, there are opportunities for individuals to assume roles of leadership, training, support, and policy making that are broader than the ascribed roles of "parent" or "teacher" or "administrator."

8. A "COMMUNITY AS NETWORK OF RELATIONSHIPS" PERSPECTIVE

The eighth point of the transition concerns what really cements the partnership between school personnel and non–school personnel—building community through our actual physical presence in the schools. The participants in partner schools are adamant and clear about this being the essential ingredient for cementing the partnership—that university and other non–school personnel spend time in the schools and in settings with children—Murrell's (1991) notion of "being there." The measure of our success as agents for change is not the *expertise* we bring as university people, but rather our *capacity to learn in the company of others.* This vision engenders an active disbelief in deficit-based professional practice that targets "clients" as needy, pathological, and incompetent. This vision calls us to foster relational practices in our personal and professional interactions and in our invitations to those with whom we work.

9. A "JOINT RESPONSIBILITY AND ACCOUNTABILITY" PERSPECTIVE

Responsibility and accountability must be shared by all members of the partnership. University *responsibility* means university and college partners sharing the responsibility for the gains in academic achievement and personal development of children in those communities and *accountability* for lack of progress.

SUMMARY

There is a crisis of knowledge inherent in the movement to renew urban schools through collaborative partnerships devoted to improving the quality of teachers and teaching. The crisis is multifaceted, existing in large-scale relationships between practitioners and policy makers as well as among university, school, and community partners. The challenge is how to grapple with the tasks of redeveloping teacher education without losing sight of the facets of knowledge that are critical to success.

This chapter illustrated the complexity of the challenges posed through a case study and introduced nine features of an urban-focused, community-dedicated, and practice-oriented approach to collaborative renewal of urban schools. In the next chapter, I more specifically detail the conceptual framework for this collaborative renewal.

CHAPTER 2

The Contexts for Improving the Quality of Urban Teaching in Partnership

To understand the teacher's teaching, it is important to understand [the] circumstances, to understand the context *in which the teacher works. We need to know how the teacher's environment influences the teacher's teaching. We need an* ecological *understanding of teaching—of how teaching develops to suit the environment, and in what ways we can and should change that environment if we want to change what goes on there.*

—*M. Fullan and A. Hargreaves,*
What's Worth Fighting for in Your School?

TEACHING CAN BE A REMARKABLY SOLITARY and isolated professional activity, whether based in the school or in the university (Lortie, 1975). Although no one would disagree that collaboration among educators from universities, schools, and neighborhoods is essential for quality education, remarkably little headway has been made in organizing institutional systems of collaboration. Public school administration, for the most part, does not develop the professional abilities of its teachers—certainly not in relation to professional abilities of collaborative work, which are arguably essential for effective work in underresourced urban public schools.

In most school systems professional development still consists of a set of courses or discrete workshop experiences. There is little expectation of improved practice as a result of an inservice experience. The requirement

35

placed on teachers is not a demonstration of improved or more accomplished practice, but rather the documentation of a certain number of points amassed on the basis of attendance at any of a wide array of inservice workshops and other "professional experiences." In short, professional development rarely elevates practice because it is not expected to. Further, it is rarely linked to practice, since professional experiences are usually one-shot stand-alone "workshops" that carry no expectation of a sustained effort on the part of participants. The measure of a good "inservice" at this level, from the perspective of teachers, is whether they can walk away with at least one technique or material that they modify for use in their own teaching the next day.

The lack of *development of the practice* of preservice and first-year teachers is a long-standing and widely acknowledged problem in teacher education. The absence of a system of support and development for first-year teachers has led to sizable attrition among those entering the profession (Darling-Hammond, 1997; Lortie, 1975). The ineffective teaching of novice teachers and the instabilities of turnover compound the legacy of scarce intellectual and material resources in urban schools, and many leave the teaching profession within the first 3 years. In the latter instance, whatever valuable practical knowledge new teachers may have gained as they grappled with the challenges of their urban practice during their short tenure is lost in the wake of their departure from teaching.

This chapter articulates the idea of the *community of practice for the development of accomplished practice* for teachers, particularly for urban teachers, and how that community might be instrumental in developing collaborative cultures. From the perspective of professional development, a community of practice should give beginning teachers the best possible opportunity to improve their practice. More specifically, such a community of practice is an alternative to the basic working arrangement for induction of new teachers, interns, and student teachers—the *clinical triad* (Murrell, 1998).

Briefly, the clinical triad consists of a university supervisor, a cooperating teacher, and a student teacher or intern. It is a basic arrangement in virtually every program of teacher preparation involving a clinical experience or practicum for student teachers and interns. The basic relationship is one of providing assistance and guidance to the novice teacher. The clinical triad is the foundation of the university–school connection in the professional development schools (PDS) model of partnership collaboration as well as in other types of partnerships between schools of education and public schools.

A significant body of research indicates that the clinical triad does not provide sufficient opportunities for beginning teachers to reflect on the problems of teaching and to transform issues that appear problematic into rich opportunities for learning (Darling-Hammond, 1992; Goodlad, 1994). This problem is particularly the case in urban schools, where there are comparatively fewer resources (Liston & Zeichner, 1991). Improving on this basic set of relations requires a deeper inquiry into three levels of practice (Murrell, 1998): (1) a micro level addressing development of the individual learners in classroom contexts; (2) a meso level addressing development of the relationships constituting the social, cultural, and professional fabric of the school community; and (3) a macro level addressing development of broader institutional, neighborhood, family, and other support systems. Note the emphasis on *development* in each.

The task of enriching the set of professional working relationships between schools of education and public schools might be described as building a *community of practice* (Lave, 1988) or a *circle of practice* (Murrell, in press). Both of these theoretical frameworks employ a common set of concepts, including the notion of an *activity setting* (Tharp & Gallimore, 1991). They are similar to the idea of *collaborative cultures* as discussed in school change literature (cf. Hargreaves & Fullan, 1996; Nias, Southworth, & Yeomans, 1989).

ACTIVITY SETTINGS OF PRACTICE

In everyday language, an activity setting is a specific situational context that is recognizable and familiar to the participants, who come to the setting with an understanding of the appropriate roles and rules of interaction. There are *instructional activity settings,* such as reading groups, show-and-tell, and morning meeting. There are also *professional activity settings,* such as staff meetings, inservice workshops, and curriculum retreats. The important idea, however, is that the setting involves a shared purposive endeavor, carried out in a framework of commonly held cultural assumptions, expectations, and practices. The clinical triad is a professional activity setting for which the shared purposive endeavor is the training of the student teacher or intern.

The term *activity setting* denotes the unit of analysis for unpacking the social, cultural, and interactional context for both teacher development and student achievement. To organize a community of practice, participants in a partnership need to be able to analyze and assess the activity settings of their shared professional work. We will turn to communities of practice after a brief discussion of the most common activity settings in school–university partnerships—the clinical triad (Murrell, 1998).

CLINICAL TRIAD

As mentioned above, the *clinical triad* is a professional activity setting that exists in virtually every school–university arrangement for student teaching (see Figure 2.1). The triad's three participants are the university clinical supervisor (usually a faculty member representing the teacher education program), a cooperating teacher, and the student teacher or intern. In many cases, the clinical supervisor from the university also runs a concurrent seminar for the student teacher, and other student teachers, to debrief and process their practice. The role of the clinical supervisor is to organize the collaboration with the cooperating teacher and the student teacher. The role of the cooperating teacher is to assist the developing practice of the student teacher.

The set of practices of the clinical triad is devoted to the development of the teaching proficiencies of the student teacher or intern. The clinical experience or practicum, in most cases, involves a minimum of three three-

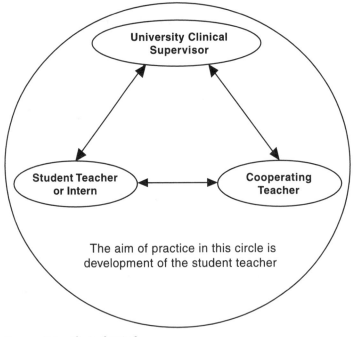

FIGURE 2.1. Clinical Triad

way conferences or meetings, at which the teaching performance of the candidate is evaluated according to criteria or standards set by the teacher education program.

In this setting, the cooperating teacher and the university clinical supervisor are conjointly responsible for both formative and summative assessment of the candidate's teaching practice. The assessment of a student teacher's progress is supposed to be made according to clear performance criteria. Usually, the unit (teacher preparation program) has incorporated state-mandated performance standards with those provided to the clinical supervisor and the cooperating teacher to use in evaluating the progress and success of the student teacher.

There are several reasons why the clinical triad is *not* the appropriate activity setting in which to expect that "critical inquiry into teaching practice" will take place, as proclaimed by advocates of the PDS model. Most importantly, the principal aim of certifying the practice of the candidate is often at odds with the aims requiring analyses and interrogation of classroom instructional practices. For example, the summative assessment of the candidate's readiness to teach cannot easily be carried out at the same time the cooperating teacher's assessment criteria are being questioned. Hence, on one level there is the issue of raising the ire of the cooperating teacher, upon whom the clinical supervisor depends to "sign off" on the candidate. The tasks of formative and summative assessment of the candidate may leave less room for interrogating a wider range of practices.

On a deeper level, the college supervisor may have serious concerns about the *instructional activity settings*—the approaches, philosophies, and instructional delivery system of the cooperating teacher or the school. Further, these issues may be out of reach of any systematic interrogation without subverting the system of assistance for the student teacher. Critical interrogation could create an "uncooperative" cooperating teacher. Because of this, the critical input provided by the university side of the partnership ought to be in a context that is broader than that of the clinical triad. This broader context or setting is called a *professional activity setting*. This context of professional activity should include, but not be limited to, the consideration of the instructional practice of both the student teacher and the cooperating teacher.

There are at least two ways in which the clinical triad could be enhanced as an activity setting for the development of practice as a result of the school–university partnership. One of these is a greater interrogation of teaching and learning, making the clinical triad both an *instructional* and *professional activity setting*. This means that both the clinical supervisor and the cooperating teacher would expand their roles to include being investigators of the teaching and learning. The result might be a circle of practice that develops not only the practice of the student teacher but also the instructional practices of the school. This is, in fact, one of the aims that the original Holmes Group (now the Holmes Partnership) had in mind with the first proposals of the professional development school more than 15 years ago.

The second means of improving on the clinical triad through school–university partnership is related to the first. Interrogation of practice in the clinical experience could be opened up with the involvement of other participants—university faculty, parents, and other stakeholders—again making the clinical triad (or quadrad or quintad) into both an *instructional* and *professional activity setting*. Specifically, suppose there were professional space in which the classroom teacher, the university supervisor, the student teacher, and an arts and sciences faculty person from the university could develop the richness and quality of instruction. Then there could be the development of appropriately mutual concerns—the quality of the student teacher's development and the quality of instruction in classroom.

CIRCLE OF PRACTICE

The notion of a *circle of practice* (see Figure 2.2) illustrates the relationship between college and school partners that permits interrogation of practice in professional activity settings. A circle of practice is a group of individuals bound together in a mutual activity with mutual exchange of ideas, values, and actions toward a common purpose or set of purposes. This is represented in Figure 2.2 by the participants in the clinical triad (i.e., university clinical supervisor, student teacher, and cooperating teacher) and by the participants outside the triad (i.e., arts and sciences faculty, parents, and community-based educators).

In Figure 2.2, the central circle shows again the clinical triad, but in relation to a broader set of participants. The central circle that encompasses the clinical triad represents the social sphere of activity and interaction in the learning community between a beginning and experienced teacher. The cooperating teacher's role in the activity setting consists of actions that assist the student teacher's practice, such as giving feedback, providing guidance, and explaining practice. The student teacher's role in this setting is to develop the knowledge-in-use required for becoming a more proficient teacher. In addition to this, however, others who are not participants in the clinical triad can play assisting roles. This wider circle is referred to as a circle of practice.

Years ago, I spent a week working in Westside Preparatory Academy in Chicago, one of the schools that Marva Collins established. One of my

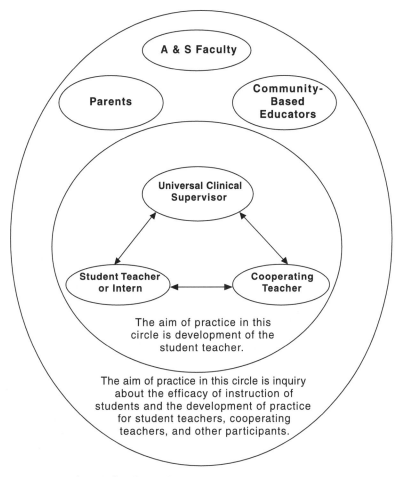

FIGURE 2.2. The Circle of Practice

most enduring images of the classrooms there was the row of parents sitting in the back of the classroom as instruction was going on. These parents nodded assent when the young instructor seemed to be doing a particularly good job of interacting with the children in the course of instruction. The young teachers received immediate, concurrent, and ongoing feedback based on these nonverbal cues. The presence of parents in the instructional circles of the school is a good example of this wider circle of practice; it is also an illustration that one need not be a "pedagogical expert" to contribute to the quality of instructional practice.

A circle of practice ought to have a clearly defined purpose. For example, a circle of practice devoted to elevating the quality of the literacy learning programs at a school might involve any number of teachers, university people, parents, and other educators. However, this enclave of practitioners working on literacy cannot be too far removed from the actual instructional activity setting—teachers and children learning together in classrooms.

COMMUNITY OF PRACTICE AND ACTION TEAMS

A *community of practice* is the term we have given to the type of working teams, or *action teams*, we are striving for in our partnerships (see Figure 2.3). We might regard it as a coordinated collection of several circles of practice. Alternatively, we might view it as single circle of practice with multiple purposes—for example, developing novice teachers, instituting a new mathematics curriculum in the school, or improving the collaboration of university and school faculty.

In any event, a community of practice is a group of individuals bound together in a mutual activity with mutual exchange of ideas, values, and actions toward a common purpose or set of purposes. We assume those purposes to be quality teaching and learning. However, the idea of a community of practice encompasses much more than an action team or committee. This is a group that creates a new common space—a new context of professional activity where the interests of people in higher education, parents, school people, and other personnel come together. In this new common space the practices and policies of the school are interrogated in the interest of creating the conditions for a quality education for all children.

There are three key qualities of a community of practice: (1) There is mutual engagement in joint activities, such as curriculum development, school problem solving, and day-to-day instruction. (2) There is a shared repertoire of practices that are continuously revised in light of experience and inquiry. (3) There is a commitment to the development of systems that promote development of learners and practitioners, learners *as* practitioners, and practitioners *as* learners.

In general terms, the purpose of *action teams* is to create a community of practice. A circle of practice is meant to involve parents and educators from community organizations as critical and collaborative decision makers in the development of accomplished practice.

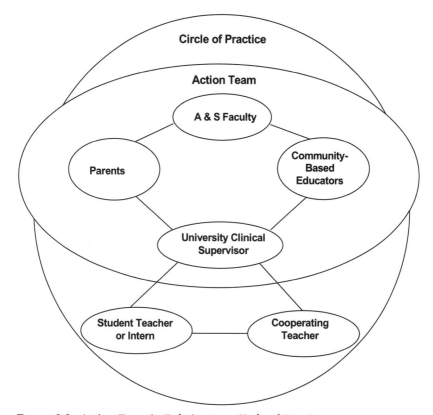

FIGURE 2.3. Action Team in Relation to a Circle of Practice

A common value held by successful circles of practice is that there are no experts in universal practice. That is, expertise is developed in collaborative work; it is not something that a select few "bring to the table." The system of practice must emerge from authentic work, respectful collaboration, and the humility of good anthropology (Meier, 1982) in fulfilling the aims of quality urban education. This means the development of a network of practice in place of the old clinical triad model. A circle of practice should provide rich supportive networks for beginning teachers that address their professional isolation; it should also provide a means of overcoming the cultural encapsulation of cooperating teachers and beginning teachers alike.

ACTION TEAMS FOR BUILDING
COLLABORATIVE PARTNERSHIP

Building and establishing a circle of practice is easy to espouse in theory, and many scholars of teacher education recognize that creating some form of a *professional learning community* is absolutely necessary. The actual work of creating these new networks of support is difficult and demanding— and very unlikely considering the way in which professional development schools operate currently. This work requires patience, compromise, and a readiness to reexamine long-held assumptions so as to advance the work of improving teacher quality and student achievement in urban schools, something rarely taken on in professional development schools. The notion of an action team represents a new arrangement within which all members of the community partnership can collaborate.

THE CONTINUUM OF COMMUNITY
PARTNERSHIP DEVELOPMENT

To be a contributing factor in elevating the quality of teachers and education, particularly in urban contexts, collaborative partnerships must be organized in ways that really focus on the development of accomplished practice. Accomplished practice, in this account, means not only research on and development of effective pedagogy but also demonstrable yields in the achievement and development of children.

Figure 2.4 depicts a continuum along which different types of partnership arrangements can be placed according to their degree of commitment to the development of urban practice. The continuum is based on the degree to which a school and university together address the nine aims of developing practice (Murrell & Borunda, 1998). Principal among these qualities is authentic, jointly engaged, meaningful practice that elevates student achievement and supports development. This framework will be used in Chapter 10 to elaborate on and summarize the steps in building a community-dedicated and practice-oriented teacher preparation partnership among schools, universities, and communities. For now, I wish to illustrate the pathway of change.

PATH OF CHANGE TOWARD PARTNERSHIP
IN TEACHER PREPARATION

The next stage in the development of a collaborative partnership is a circle of practice. When the collaboration based on extensive student teacher or

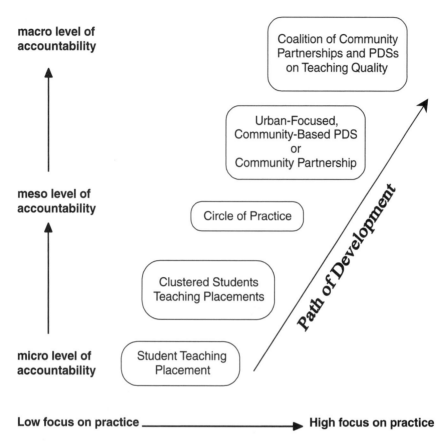

macro level of accountability

Coalition of Community Partnerships and PDSs on Teaching Quality

Urban-Focused, Community-Based PDS or Community Partnership

meso level of accountability

Circle of Practice

Clustered Students Teaching Placements

micro level of accountability

Student Teaching Placement

Path of Development

Low focus on practice ⟶ High focus on practice

FIGURE 2.4. Continuum of Partnerships by Level of Accountability and Commitment to Developing Practice

internship placement arrangements evolves to conversations of how these arrangements might extend to inquiry and the *development of accomplished practice*, it becomes a circle of practice. The second stage in the development of a collaborative partnership is the extension of a *circle of practice* to a *community of practice*. In other words, we might think of a community of practice as multiple circles of practice—multiple contexts in which university faculty, school faculty, parents, and interested others are engaged in an activity to enhance instructional practice or professional practice.

The key diagram for this last discussion is Figure 2.4. The diagram represents a progression of development of school–university partnerships on two dimensions. On the horizontal dimension is the commitment to practice. More specifically, it represents the degree of joint accountability for the development of accomplished practices for elevating the academic achievement and personal development of children. On the left-hand side of the diagram is a lesser commitment to the practices that elevate school achievement (i.e., single student teacher placement). On the right-hand side is a higher commitment to such accomplished practice (i.e., coalitions devoted to elevating teacher quality and student achievement).

The second dimension in the diagram refers to the levels of organizational accountability and professional activity—the micro, meso, and macro levels of professional activity settings. In the diagram, the bottom represents the micro level of professional activity. The middle of the continuum, containing the *circles of practice* type of partnership, is at the meso level of professional activity settings. The top of the diagram represents the macro, or interinstitutional, level of professional activity, including community partnerships and networks of partnerships.

This continuum could be viewed as a model representing the progressive development of a school–university partnership. The trajectory of development ranges from a limited level of school–university involvement (i.e., student teacher placement) to a fully integrated professional development school (i.e., a school conjointly operated by school and university partners). Higher joint accountability for, and with, communities and families characterizes those collaborative partnerships toward the right-hand portion of the developmental trajectory. A lab school might occupy the far right end on the basis of the integration of practices, if it were not for the problem of including the wider community. A lab school certainly has a greater likelihood of consolidating and coordinating instructional activity, but not necessarily a greater likelihood of demanding a high accountability to students, parents, and community.

By placing these types of collaborative partnerships side by side on a continuum of the degree of collaboration, common inquiry into practice, and joint accountability to student achievement and community participation, it is easier to visualize the development of a partnership.

While placing a cluster of student teachers in a school barely seems to constitute a partnership because it lacks shared responsibility for student achievement, it nonetheless does represent some kind of preliminary agreement about the development of practice. A cluster placement of student teachers is an advance over placement of a single student teacher in that it represents a greater commitment to the development of practice.

The *circles of practice* level of collaboration between a school and university, depicted in the middle portion of the diagram, represents still higher accountability and joint determination of accomplished practice in instruction and professional activity. A joint commitment to practice and to student achievement is what differentiates a partnership with clustered placements from a partnership that has developed a true collaborative practice and inquiry in the circle of practice. Recall also that neither of these arrangements—*clustered placements* or a *circle of practice*—requires a contractual agreement between the school and the university, beyond that required to place student teachers or interns.

There are many other forms a circle of practice can take apart from the clinical triad. Funded curriculum projects, study groups, and professional development projects are all activities that might involve both school and university faculty without the necessity of a contractual agreement of partnership between the two. In relation to the continuum, a PDS is a school–university collaboration in which all these activities *are* contractually specified in a formal agreement.

In Chapter 10, I return to this continuum to summarize the framework and the practices necessary to effect change from traditional models of teacher preparation to effective partnerships.

SUMMARY

The chapter introduced the conceptual underpinnings for a practice-oriented, urban-focused, and community-dedicated framework for a professional unit to prepare urban educators. The framework calls for the development and mobilization of human systems involving university, community, and school personnel working collaboratively to elevate teaching practice. These new enclaves of practice were given specific names—*circle of practice* and *community of practice*—based on the level and type of activity with respect to the institutions and organizations involved.

The concepts of the *circle of practice* and *accomplished practice of the community teacher* describe the micro level and meso level of practice in the development of a school–university partnership that fully addresses the challenges of urban education. In the next chapter, this model of the circle of practice is elaborated as the schema for building a university–community–school partnership for the development of quality teaching. Chapter 4 then illustrates this development.

CHAPTER 3

Community Teachers— The New Model of Urban Teacher Preparation

Some may object to blending together diverse issues of aims, structure, status and vulnerability, institutional linkages, career development, governance and change strategies. We teacher educators have come used to addressing these issues one at a time or, at most, in clusters of two or three. However, unless one concurrently considers normative, structural, personnel, institutional, career, any effort to reform teacher education will be incomplete and therefore deeply at risk.
—*A. R. Tom*, Redesigning Teacher Education

THE LAST CHAPTER INTRODUCED the conceptual underpinnings for a practice-oriented, urban-focused, and community-dedicated framework for the preparation of urban educators. The framework calls for the development and mobilization of new human systems of practice by which university, community, and school personnel work collaboratively to elevate teaching quality and groom accomplished urban teachers. My purpose in this chapter is to elaborate the conceptual framework by illustrating it as a strategy working in synchrony with the national agenda for improving the quality of teaching.

BRINGING TOGETHER DIFFERENT LEVELS
OF TEACHER PREPARATION

How do levels of activity—in classrooms, in professional development, in policy making—come together into a single system for producing good teachers? I have already discussed two components of that system—the *clinical triad* and the broader more inclusive *circle of practice*. These two ideas represent two levels of professional teaching practice at the micro level and the meso level, respectively. A third level of professional practice— the *community of practice*—constitutes a macro level involving institutional and policy concerns. The macro level of practice subsumes the other two—the consideration of classroom practice (micro level) and the inter-professional collaboration for developing systems of inquiry and practice (meso level). I turn now to how all three levels fit together as a system for preparing good teachers.

Normally, an analysis of the macro-level concerns of a school–university partnership would require a discussion of the interinstitutional and ideological issues present in teacher preparation programs, state regulations, and federal requirements as they relate to school improvement. However, movements afoot in this country have already considerably shaped this analysis and discussion. I refer here to the national agenda for reforming schools through the improvement of teaching, initiated by the National Commission on Teaching and America's Future (NCTAF) and animated by Section 202 (Title II) of Congress's reauthorization of the Education Act in 1998. Taken together, they shape a national agenda with seven aims:

- Get serious about standards for both students and teachers.
- Reinvent teacher preparation and professional development.
- Fix teacher recruitment, and put qualified teachers in every classroom.
- Encourage and reward teacher knowledge and skill.
- Create schools that are organized for student and teacher success.
- Support with grants the development of new and effective urban teacher education programs that involve collaborative partnership among higher education, communities, high-need neighborhoods, and K–12 schools.
- Hold teacher preparation institutions accountable and close those that do not meet objective criteria of effectiveness.

In virtually every articulation of this new national agenda (e.g., the NCTAF report and the federal Title II legislation), the school–university partnership is considered a linchpin in school reform. For example, funding for teacher recruitment grants and teacher quality grants requires that the grantee be a part of a collaborative partnership that involves a university and a school or school system in a high-need area. Most important, though, is the fact that the new national agenda of education reform requires and expects a synthesis of efforts and energies of professionals from micro, meso, and macro levels of activity. The new national agenda expects teacher preparation to change in ways that require an interdependence of the efforts to improve classroom practice, to improve interprofessional collaboration, to enrich professional development, and to reorganize institutional activity.

A BLUEPRINT FOR PREPARING COMMUNITY TEACHERS

The community partnership framework presented in these pages provides a blueprint for urban teacher preparation in synchrony with the national agenda for improving the quality of teaching. The framework presented here embodies a critique of the professional development school (PDS) model of school–university partnership, which is one of the implicit requirements of the national agenda. The criticism is that the PDS model privileges the partnership between higher education and schools, to the exclusion of other equally important partners such as parent groups, community-based agencies, and neighborhood groups. In terms of the framework, the issue for the PDS approach to partnership is how to develop inclusive and appropriate circles of practice.

Preparing teachers for accomplished practice in urban contexts requires a continuous interrogation of the role that public schools, the current reform movements, and bureaucratic structures (such as PDSs) play in the perpetuation of societal stratification and social inequities. Without this critical perspective, it would be next to impossible for school–university partnerships to formulate practice that effects systemic change at all levels (i.e., micro, meso, and macro) of practice. Human systems and institutions that do not systemically question their fundamental assumptions, values, and goals undoubtedly contribute to the perpetuation of structural inequality.

Although the track record that PDS enterprises have in this type of critical inquiry thus far has not been good (Murrell, 1998), there are reasons to expect that the PDS movement will promote the development of more effective models of school–university–community collaboration. To begin with, the number of teacher education programs associated with PDSs is dramatically increasing. Currently, according to Abdal-

Haqq (1998), about half of the nation's teacher preparation institutions are aligned with professional development schools. A second reason is the National Council for the Accreditation of Teacher Education's (NCATE) development of PDS standards, which offer the hope of quality assurances in the formation of inclusive, fair, and authentic working relationships.

Still required, however, is a critical, cultural, and analytical perspective in the development of partnerships, which is the weak link in the development of PDSs (Murrell, 1998). Critical consideration of the cultural, historical, and political dimensions of urban education are essential to the successful preparation of accomplished urban teachers. In some ways, developing this critical perspective in practice is the most important task in the formation of partnerships among community, school, and university. Said another way, the primary challenge of PDSs is to develop an appropriate community of practice.

Evidence that this happens systematically in professional development school is virtually nonexistent in the educational literature. There is scant research that interrogates whether PDSs provide those new material resources, curricular innovations, and instructional approaches that actually lead to enhanced learning and development among children of color. However, this does not mean that a PDS-type partnership cannot eventually meet these needs.

MEETING THE CHALLENGE

The challenge in the preparation of urban teachers for the renewal of urban public schools might be thought of as encompassing three concurrent aims. The first aim is working toward mobilizing *communities of practice*—communities of cooperative effort, learning, and shared practice. The second aim is working to increase the number of *community teachers*—teachers of color with the ability and experience to work effectively with students from diverse communities. The third aim is developing the *conceptual and cultural integrity of pedagogical knowledge*—finding ways to draw on emergent local knowledge of successful pedagogy for human development in the community of learning/practice.

WHAT IS A COMMUNITY TEACHER?

The first aim, that of building new *communities of practice*, is the *process*. The *product*, if you will, is the *community teacher*. The revision of teacher preparation for the renewal of urban schools depends on providing enough community teachers. What exactly is a *community teacher?*

A community teacher is one who possesses contextualized knowledge of the culture, community, and identity of the children and families he or she serves and draws on this knowledge to create the core teaching practices necessary for effectiveness in diverse setting. In contrast to a course-based teacher preparation curriculum, this is a special knowledge-in-use that shows up in teachers' ability to forge strong connections with children in diverse community settings as they elicit development and achievement in real practice. A significant part of this contextualized pedagogical knowledge is the candidate's own cultural, political, and racial identity. The extent to which candidates can critically develop their own "positionality" determines how central or peripheral a role they play in the development and academic achievement of children, youth, and families in diverse urban communities.

There are many excellent illustrations of this community teacher idea in the work of, for example, Foster (1997), Ladson-Billings (1994), and Lee (1994) regarding the qualities of Black artful teaching style, culturally relevant teaching, and African-centered pedagogy, respectively. The reader is encouraged to examine this work for characterizations of the community teacher in settings that are predominantly African American. My task here is to explain the community teacher in more generic terms and to show that the cultural knowledge and shared cultural identity the community teacher needs to work with urban children, families, and communities can be developed. Consider the following scenarios.

Scenario One took place in a first-grade, predominantly African American classroom. It was morning, just after the children had arrived and just prior to sharing circle. The European American candidate had just begun her third field experience, her last practicum course before student teaching. She has long, straight, blonde hair and was sitting on the rug. Astride her were two African American girls who were stroking and playing with her hair. The African American cooperating teacher had observed this on two prior occasions but said nothing. On this day, however, she called the candidate aside and asked her not to allow the children to play with her hair. The candidate responded first by saying, "It's OK, I don't mind." The cooperating teacher responded firmly, "It's *not* OK, and it is not whether you mind or not that makes it OK or not OK."

Scenario Two took place in a second-grade classroom that was half European American and half African American. One of the reading groups was conducted by a student teacher who was being observed by her college supervisor. The candidate was engaging and warm in her interactions with children. However, the college supervisor noticed and documented that the candidate uniformly failed to call on the African American children in the group, even though their hands were up as often as the hands of the others. In a group of seven children, neither the two African American girls nor the African American boy were called on. Over the course of the reading group, their attempts to be called on dramatically increased, with the utterances of "Ooh! Ooh!" as they waved their hands frantically. In the final phase of the reading group, their efforts to be called on had all but disappeared. When the college supervisor brought this to the attention of the European American candidate in the postconference, the candidate only then realized that she had not been aware of either her preferential treatment of the European American children or the diminished participation of the African American children. The cooperating teacher, who was also European American and who had not noticed this preferential pattern either, said of the candidate at last, "Oh well, she is doing her best." The college supervisor firmly replied, "Well, as far as this pattern goes, her best is not going to be good enough."

Scenario Three took place at the university's college of education, where a young Hispanic social studies middle school teacher had excitedly accepted a position as a clinical faculty member. Through a special arrangement of the professional development school, he was able to take a 1-year leave of absence to teach the middle school social studies methods course and to serve as clinical faculty for student teachers, interns, and field students at his middle school. At first he really enjoyed his status as the first experimental clinical faculty member. But by the Thanksgiving break, he felt overwhelmed by the things he had been asked to do. Since being at the university he had been asked to sit on the Multicultural Committee, the Minority Recruitment Committee, and the Steering Committee of the Institute for Cultural Studies. He was also asked to mentor two Hispanic education students and to referee three conflicts between faculty and students that had racial overtones. When he took his concern to the dean, she reinforced how happy she was that he had joined the faculty, especially in light of the college's newly proclaimed commitment to diversity. The young man replied, "I don't want to seem ungrateful, but it seems that my African American colleagues and I are turning into the 'diversity franchise.' If the college really values diversity, shouldn't that commitment extend beyond the people of color that happen to be here?"

COMMUNITY TEACHER KNOWLEDGE

Each of these scenarios illustrates the particularized knowledge of the community teacher at the three different levels of practice. At the micro level of classroom dynamics and interpersonal interaction between teacher and learner, we have an instance in which a young woman does not yet have sufficient pedagogical knowledge to understand what might be problematic about letting African American girls play with her hair. Understandably, she only views the interaction as a moment of bonding and greater personal connection with the girls. She has not yet learned the situatedness of this act within the larger context of race, power, and identity development, and what a public fawning over a symbol of whiteness (blonde hair) might mean in a class of African American children. As she becomes a community teacher, she will realize the power of modeling and the potential consequences of the behavior for the audience of other African American children who are both consuming and constructing their images of what constitutes "pretty."

The community teacher is aware of and, when necessary, actively researches the knowledge traditions of the cultures represented among the children, families, and communities he or she serves. The community teacher enacts those knowledge traditions as a means of making meaningful connections for and with children and their families. It is the difference between merely holding a cultural fair to which children bring a food or an artifact "from their culture" and daily classroom experience that authentically incorporates the lives, cultures, and experiences of the learners and their families.

The second scenario is an instance of community teacher knowledge (CTK) at the meso level of instructional activity that involves both instructional practice and interprofessional collaboration. The college supervisor has the task of bringing an awareness of culturally appropriate instructional practice into the clinical triad. As you can see, this is a knowledge that is somewhat different from reading about learning styles or managing instruction. At the very least, there is a humility of good anthropology that is a part of CTK—an openness about ways of being and doing, and a tentativeness about one's assumptions and inferences about the new ways one encounters. In CTK there is also a capacity for building a shared understanding that includes an awareness of positionality of participants, especially as one enters a cultural community different from one's own. This is a knowledge-in-use that comes from a cultural and political awareness or "positionality." The college supervisor asserts CTK by reinforcing that the pattern of preferential treatment of children should not be tolerated under *any* circumstances—whether it is exhibited by an experienced or a beginning teacher. Her comments influence the practice of both the intern and the cooperating teacher

The third scenario illustrates CTK at the macro level of interinstitutional collaboration of institutional systems of practice. The young instructor struggles with the tendencies of bureaucracies to declare a commit-ment to diversity without providing the means of holding people to ac-count. As often happens without continuous development and evaluation, commitment to diversity can easily become more symbolic than substan-tive. The initiative to diversify curriculum or faculty too often becomes relegated to a new position or new office without the provision of suffi-cient institutional authority to hold people accountable. In this case, the symbols are the formation of committees and the involvement of more people of color. The presence of minority participants becomes not only the symbol of a commitment to diversity but also the assumed interven-tion itself.

In all three cases, the necessary CTK emerges from a complex mix of reflective experience, cultural knowledge, and critical inquiry. One need not be African American or Hispanic to become a *community teacher* in African American and Hispanic communities. However, as the saying goes, "it helps," because such candidates are more likely to share the lived ex-periences, cultural knowledge, and political sensibilities of the cultural communities in which they teach.

BUILDING THE SCAFFOLDING FOR CHANGE

As mentioned previously, there is virtually unanimous agreement among educational practitioners, researchers, policy analysts, and teacher edu-cators that the renewal of urban schools will require the bridging of at least two professional communities—the community of educators in schools, colleges, and departments of education on one hand, and the actual urban neighborhoods on the other hand. The challenge is in how we design *sys-tems of practice* for the collateral development of urban teacher education and urban schools.

The *community partnership*, consisting of a trilateral collaboration among community-based, university-based, and school-based partners, is one such framework. It specifically targets the shortage of Black and His-panic teachers and the impending shortage of urban teachers. An urban-focused, community-dedicated partnership operates as a compact that elicits the collaboration of community-based organizations, university personnel, public school educators, and community stakeholders toward the three aims introduced in the previous section on "Meeting the Chal-lenge." In this framework, inquiry and development in teacher prepara-tion move in two directions. Inquiry framed by the formal knowledge of such things as human learning and cognition, curriculum theory, and the liberal arts moves from university classrooms to urban neighborhoods and to programs of youth development in community locations. But critical understanding of the uses of these formal forms of knowledge also flows from practice in community settings back to the university.

The community partnership framework presented here does not pretend to be a full-blown model in the same vein as the PDS model as presented by the NCTAF, the National Center for Restructuring Education, Schools and Teaching (NCREST), the Holmes Partnership, and others. Rather it is the blueprint for an evolving system of practice for an urban-focused, community-connected, and practice-oriented program of professional development for urban educators.

The community teacher conceptual framework incorporates the same principles of an effective PDS as articulated by NCREST, the NCTAF report, and similar publications. The operating principles in the NCREST (2001) statement articulate qualities of community-building effort, such as the following:

- A partnership or collaborative develops a shared, publicly articulated vision and commitment to a set of core beliefs that apply to all learners.
- Communities of learners are forged within schools and across traditional school–community boundaries.
- The adult members of the community are engaged in systematic, collaborative, and continuous inquiry about teaching and learning.
- Members of the PDS community are committed to continual reflection, self and organizational renewal, and the pursuit of ever more powerful and inclusive approaches to supporting student success.

The real work of practice is that of building relationships across divides that inevitably exist when bureaucratic entities such as school departments and universities attempt to work with socio-organic entities such as neighborhood associations and community agencies. To a large extent the operating principles stand as unrealized ideals in the landscape of professional development schools.

BUILDING FROM PRIOR EFFORTS

The conceptual framework for a university–community–school partnership presented here is a much-needed alternative to, or perhaps an important extension of, the PDS model. It contrasts with the PDS model in three ways: (1) by refocusing the purposes of education and teacher preparation on the mobilization of resources for the development of the community; (2) by recentering the educational leadership on those with proven success in working with the most intractable, disaffected, and alienated youth in urban schools; and (3) by harvesting local professional teacher knowledge gained from ongoing successful work with urban youth.

What distinguishes a community partnership framework from the PDS approach is that the fabric of the teacher preparation program is cut from the same cloth as the professional development of all adults working with the young people. In both venues we seek to recognize and increase instances of accomplished practice as evidenced by the development and learning achievement of the children in urban neighborhoods and schools. The framework seeks a seamless connection between the education of the young people and the professional development of their teachers and mentors.

Put another way, *the development of a community teacher* necessarily involves two partnership goals. One of these is recruiting future community teachers—Black and Hispanic students who are struggling to find meaning and opportunity in education and who are beginning to see teaching as a way of being active agents in the development of their communities. The second of these is organizing adults currently working with young people in community-based programs (many of whom are working to earn teaching certification in the course of this work). The community partnership is the location where both forms of development occur.

AIMS FOR TEACHING TO DIVERSITY

Teacher preparation in a community partnership framework incorporates the NCREST principles listed above but also includes additional principles that go beyond the PDS approach in significant ways. Summarized below are the critical aims of community partnership development:

1. Development of *community teachers*—teachers, particularly teachers of color, with the ability and experience to work effectively with students from diverse communities
2. Creation of *locally centered communities of practice*—genuine communities of cooperative effort, learning, and shared practice constituted among those doing the daily work of enabling youth
3. Production of *grounded pedagogical knowledge*—surfacing and building on the cultural integrity of traditions of knowledge among the people comprising the community and harvesting valuable professional teaching knowledge through successful practice instead of generic professional standards

This third aim is particularly important in light of the importance the new national agenda gives to preparing teachers for successful work in culturally and linguistically diverse settings. An erroneous but frequently made assumption is that this preparation should primarily increase candidates' respect for and sensitivity to cultural diversity. This view equates teaching to cultural diversity with simply respecting, honoring, recognizing, or otherwise acknowledging the cultural forms of the community.

The error lies in the assumption that merely increasing their involvement with communities and families can provide the "multicultural competency" teachers need for effective practice. There are important cultural forms—such as traditions of literacy, oral literacy, and literature—that do not currently exist in either children's school or out-of-school experience. It would be a mistake to assume, for example, that the connection African American children need to make with their rich cultural heritage of literacy for liberation can be developed merely by teachers' having access to the children, their families, and their communities.

Although this connection constitutes the core of a culturally relevant education for African American children, it is not a knowledge base that we can reasonably expect individual teachers to acquire on their own no matter how many courses are added to the "multicultural core" of their teacher preparation curriculum. Making this connection requires developing a shared knowledge of what cultural and literate traditions are and what they mean.

What contexts and experiences make it possible for candidates to access cultural knowledge and understanding in a way that informs their practice? We turn now to a description of the system of practice and how it addresses the three aims. The chapter concludes with an analysis of how the conceptual framework guides professional development in connection with the renewal of urban schools and the preparation of teachers.

AIM ONE—PREPARING THE COMMUNITY TEACHER

The core of the community partnership framework is the concept of the *community teacher*. Community teachers most often are individuals who have lived and worked in the same underresourced urban neighborhoods and communities with troubled and troubling Hispanic and African American youth in a variety of capacities. Community teachers need not be people of color, but they do need to be culturally connected with the lives, heritages, and cultural forms of the children and families in the community. If they do not share cultural understanding through shared membership in a cultural community, candidates must develop this understanding through other means.

Community teachers in African American communities most often are African American or individuals who culturally identify with African Americans and exhibit the features of the Black artful teaching style (cf. Foster, 1997; Ladson-Billings, 1994; Piestrup, 1973). This means that the teacher uses forms of talk—such as telling stories or structuring classroom discourse and interaction in certain ways (e.g., call-and-response)—and other forms of expressive culture that children recognize and respond to.

Community teacher candidates, in many cases, have a track record of successful work with youth in urban communities. Most candidates are 20-something and are recognized by the community as those who are "giving back." Community teachers see themselves as change agents and, despite their own less-than-empowering experiences with schools, see education as the key to success for the young people with whom they work. Community teachers are most often products of urban environments themselves and understand firsthand the obstacles facing young people growing up in central city neighborhoods.

Community teachers often come from backgrounds similar to those of the students who are currently underserved by most urban school systems. Community teachers are often already dedicated to improving the lives of urban youth when they embark on formal preparation to become a teacher. Community teacher candidates, in most cases, have already found and developed effective ways of working with urban youth in community settings other than schools (e.g., Boys' and Girls' Clubs, YMCA, Gang Peace, and a variety of other community-based agencies). In a community teacher partnership framework, the community connectedness that these candidates bring is viewed as a valued source of local knowledge to be integrated with their teacher preparation.

At the point potential community teachers consider formal teacher preparation, they have a solid base of understanding and a legitimate critique of teacher preparation curricula. For many culturally mainstream White students from suburban backgrounds, this generally follows their first field experience in an urban setting. Whether from an urban, rural, or suburban background, community teacher candidates tend to convey their newfound enthusiasm for liberal arts education to the children and youth they work with.

Community teachers demonstrate understanding of what it means to struggle to find meaning and opportunity in the educational system. The pool of potential community teachers is comprised of young men and women who work on a daily basis with adolescents in urban settings—such as youth workers in social service agencies or community-based organizations and paraprofessional aides in urban schools.

AIM TWO–LOCALLY CENTERED
COMMUNITIES OF PRACTICE

Community building requires that all participants share a common foundation of ideas, beliefs, discourses, and stories rooted in the purposeful actions of the group. One clear lesson learned from more than a decade of PDS initiatives (Holmes Group, 1986, 1990) is that people cannot build communities merely by instituting a new set of policies, procedures, and agreements—as has too often been the way in PDS startup. According to Valli and colleagues (1997), contextual and cultural dimensions of education are rarely systematically examined in PDS work and are only peripherally related to its goals and activities. PDS work to date lacks the critical perspective on race, class, culture, and power that is necessary to build learning communities or communities of practice.

In this regard, the community partnership framework is an urban-focused, community-based extension of the PDS idea. It is the organization of a number of new systems of practice within a university–community–school partnership. This collaborative partnership operates from a much larger base than the clinical triad discussed in Chapter 2. One of the systems of practice is a core group that identifies and works with the already-shared assumptions about the purposes of school and the social-political realities of schooling for students in underresourced urban communities. This was discussed as the *action team* in Chapter 2.

The community partnership framework is also founded on a critical interrogation of curriculum, policies, and practices in order to reconcile the divergences between the African American cultural heritage and mainstream American culture. The task of developing responsive pedagogy for African American children and other children of color involves confronting ways in which the contemporary mores of schooling contradict those in the African American heritage of education. In the community partnership framework, it is in a circle of practice that individuals successfully grapple with these issues and develop appropriate educational practices.

A brief example of this involves the conflict posed to a largely African American school community by "rugged individualism"—a cultural value that is very much a part of mainstream American culture. Along with "competition," the cultural value of "individualism" is very much part of how academic success is viewed in American popular and institutional culture. It is the Horatio Alger myth of rugged individualism and pulling oneself up by one's bootstraps (see Comer, 1997, for a discussion of this American myth). It is a powerful myth that permeates our ideology about the purposes of school and that has been turned viciously on America's "have-nots" (see Comer's discussion of this point).

The conflict comes when this cultural value, held by White and/or culturally mainstream educators, conflicts, for example, with the Africanist cultural value of "we-ness" in academic achievement. The conflict in cultural values is problematized in a community-centered approach so that students and their teachers interrogate the purposes of education. The purpose of education for children of color is to contrast their own Horatio Alger narrative of achievement with that of the historical narrative of Black achievement.

The distinguishing issue is the question of "achievement toward what end?" The response from the Horatio Alger narrative is material success, "making it," getting a slice of the American Dream, becoming comfortably middle-class. The end point is seen as becoming a member in good standing of the consumer culture. This commodification of success—represented in the frequently used phrase "giving back to the community"—is a projection of the mainstream cultural value *by* the cultural mainstream onto Black and Hispanic youth who have very different ideas about why they want a good education. The projection of the Horatio Alger "success narrative" onto those who "make it out" of the ghettos and barrios (to become participants in the consumer culture) is problematic for determining what constitutes good teaching.

AIM THREE—HARVESTING ACCOMPLISHED PRACTICE

The advocates of the NCTAF report are correct in viewing the improvement of teaching and preparation of teachers as central to the renewal of urban schools. But they are wrong to suggest, given the current configuration of public school policy and the cultural values of schooling in America, that we can synthesize and standardize effective teaching practice in diverse urban communities through PDS training of teachers. Unless the contexts in which teachers are prepared reflect the tasks they will face as urban educators, no degree of teacher professionalization will make a difference in the quality of urban schools.

Given the many powerful articulations of pedagogy for African American children that exist (e.g., Delpit, 1996; Foster, 1997; Ladson-Billings, 1994; Shujaa, 1994), why is it that educators working with these children have not been more effective? There is a cultural integrity in the way that African American families and communities construe quality education, exemplary teachers, and academic achievement that is not captured by professional teaching standards. In the cultural heritage of African Americans, views on school achievement are not necessarily consistent with the "standard model." For example, the African American cultural heritage does not prefer "rugged individualism" and academic competition to the values of unity and the collective development of the community's intellectual resources. It is a heritage that measures the development of the individual in terms of intellect, capability, and character rather than in terms of scores on pencil-and-paper standardized tests. Therefore, building a successful community of practice in a school populated predominantly by African American children often requires a critical redefinition of what the educational establishment deems good teaching.

The problem of the movement toward professional standards on this account, as I have discussed elsewhere (Murrell, 1991, 1998), is that the standards of teaching proficiency do not adequately tap the culturally and intellectually situated teacher proficiencies required for effective work in African American and Hispanic communities. It is a problem of requiring standard proficiencies for nonstandard teaching contexts. Conceptualizing, articulating, and codifying features of exemplary practice apart from their influence in a community means that the teaching standards that teachers must meet are insufficient to the task of becoming an effective teacher.

In terms of preparing teachers for effective work in culturally diverse populations, this is a serious problem. Who is the community defining the standards of teacher competence? Is the national movement codifying codes of practice that are insufficient for effective work in diverse urban communities? How much of what is deemed "standard" meets the standard of good practice in communities with a long, powerful, intact heritage of educational achievement? The issue here is essentially a problem of validity—the question of whether teaching practices that are taken as necessary and effective in one context prove to be so when applied in another context.

These are serious questions that are being addressed by developers of performance standards for teaching competence (e.g., the Equity Panel of the Interstate New Teacher Assessment and Support Consortium). Unfortunately, there has not been very much progress in successfully integrating performance standards and assessment of accomplished practice into either urban teacher preparation or partnership work. As of this writing, only a handful of states have even attempted a performance-based system of teacher assessment. There is a severe need to make the development of local professional knowledge in urban teaching a priority in the development of accomplished teaching standards

Community nomination (Foster, 1997) is an example of how accomplished practice among diverse urban populations might be accessed, in contradistinction to the portfolio-based and performance-standards-driven articulation of exemplary teaching. It is a selection process developed by Foster (1997) for identifying exemplary teachers through direct contact with individual Black communities. The question asked in community nomination—"Whom does the community recognize as an exemplary teacher?"—is the question answered by a public recognition of such persons in the community. Analogous to community nomination is the identification of the community teacher.

CASE TWO

BACKGROUND

This case illustration is situated in the formation of a community partnership between a new school of urban education at a local university, urban schools in the neighborhoods surrounding the university, and community-based agencies and organizations that worked with children in these neighborhoods. The episodes described in this case follow on the heels of the events described in Case One involving the Martin Luther King Pilot School.

At about the time of the incidents described in Case One, Regional University (a pseudonym) inaugurated a new school of education. At the urging of the president, the provost, the dean, and an array of community organization heads and directors, the university launched the school of education with a convocation that simultaneously announced its opening and conducted a citywide agenda-setting conference. The invitation list included educators, policy makers, lawmakers, teachers, parents, and everyone else interested in and dedicated to exploring new approaches to urban education. The convocation included workshops and a networking luncheon in addition to a dedication ceremony. With this convocation event, Regional University opened the doors to a new school of urban education that proclaimed a practice-oriented, urban-focused, and community-dedicated mission.

The new school of education began expanding its relationships with community-based agencies by exploring the possibilities for developing teacher preparation for community teachers. One of the community-based agencies was a youth center based in a large housing development adjacent to the university. The Park Haven Community Center (a pseudonym) developed an after-school program in conjunction with a grant from a private foundation. The private foundation grant was awarded jointly to the university and the community-based center (CBC) for the purpose of expanding community partnerships in the areas of education, health, and human welfare. Although the grant was made to the university, the funds were administered by the center. The purpose of the grant was to "improve outcomes for students in the metropolitan public school districts and at the university and to restructure the preparation of teachers and the university faculty's way of interacting with community-based teaching and learning."

Because the grant was designed to transform the way that universities, schools, and health-care providers provided opportunities for community-based teaching and learning, it brought together people from a variety of venues who were interested in community development. For the university, this meant expanding the array of "service learning" projects that many departments and colleges within the university conducted to connect academic learning with community interest. As community and university people came together more often on self-sustaining community development initiatives, individuals on both sides who were interested in community development and urban education began to connect more and more often.

Through this initiative to preservice teachers in community settings, the university took the first steps in transforming its program of teacher preparation. The initiative created a new community-centered circle of practice. The working group, including Mr. Zed and Ms. Kay (from Case One), began by altering the early experiences of potential education students so that they would all be in community-based settings. The reasoning was that students who experience teaching and learning in community contexts would be more likely to understand the community's interests, needs, and requirements for good education. Thus university students might not become so quickly immersed in the traditional routines and practices of school life without first developing the critical interpretative lenses with which to interrogate them.

READING CIRCLE ACTIVITY LAUNCHED

The first field experience for candidates was developed in conjunction with a new community-based literacy learning program based on preparing college students to engage children in emergent literacy activity. These were developed together in order to determine the role that college students could play in the literacy learning activities of children. A scripted interactional reading activity (or instructional script) that guided the interaction of the university students with the children at the community center was developed. This reading activity script provided candidates with a framework of student–teacher interaction to elicit children's interest and immersion in literature. The instructional activity script was called the Reading Circle.

The Reading Circle paired one or two small children (kindergarten and preschool) with each university student (hereafter *candidate*), who read aloud to the children in a lap-reading format. For the early elementary children, the Reading Circle also consisted of one or two children—but the candidate could either read aloud to or read with the children, depending on whether the children were readers.

The concept of the Reading Circle emerged from collaborative work in community sites and was developed according to the needs of public school children in nonschool settings. The Reading Circle was decided on as the reading activity of candidates as a result of collaboration among the community center staff, the university liaison and director for community-based partnerships, and a public school reading specialist hired by the center. The Reading Circle was perceived to be an instructional activity setting that candidates could successfully negotiate while at the same time providing a rich literacy learning experience for the children.

VIGNETTE ONE

Sandra Hurley looked around the crowded lecture hall that seated 100 students and wondered, "Am I the only freshman?" The clatter of the movable writing tables subsided as the panel of community agency directors took their position at the front of the room. The entire class period was devoted to the community directors' presentations regarding their sites so that students in the class could make informed decisions about where they would go for their first field experience. The panel of presenters included seven directors of community-based programs and agencies.

The director of the Saturday School began the presentation with an activity. The students were asked to list things that they thought would be easy about the prospect of working in the community sites, and then to list things they thought would seem foreign and difficult. They were asked to jot down these two lists on a sheet of scrap paper. The director of the Saturday School and the director of the community literacy project then walked slowly toward the back, asking a student here and a student there to go up to the board and write one item from his or her list that was not already up there. A wave of muted giggles washed across the hall when identical "working in urban sites" appeared side by side under both the "easy" and the "foreign and difficult" categories on the board. A young man next to Sandra smiled and whispered to her, "That about sums it up!"

Sandra guessed he meant that being placed in a community-based program in an inner-city neighborhood produced ambivalent feelings— a prospect both exciting and daunting. She certainly was feeling the "daunting" part. Sandra Hurley was a feeling a little scared. She was not absolutely sure she wanted to be a teacher, much less wanted to commit to working 20 hours in the part of the city containing the most challenging contexts for teaching. She was taking this "Introduction to Education" course in order to help her decide whether she even *wanted* to be a teacher. And now she was facing the prospect of real work, with real children, alongside real professionals, with all the real responsibilities this commitment entailed.

Sandra felt particularly uneasy at the prospect of taking an active role in the teaching and development of African American children in a setting *other than* a school. At least schools seemed familiar and she had a better idea of what to expect. She could envision work in a school, with its predictable routines, rituals, and procedures. She could even envision work in an urban school, despite having grown up in a rural community. After all, she already had 12 years of experience of schools. But what was she going to do in a setting that expected her to work collaboratively with a team of parents and educators to design and implement instructional programs for children?

Sandra was having difficulty making a decision about the community site in which she would do her field placement. She realized that some of her reluctance and ambivalence was due to her lack of experience in urban environments and with African American people. When the sign-up sheets were passed out, she designated the Community Housing Development Literacy Project because she was interested in literacy development and elementary education. She was also influenced by the fact that the site was a 5-minute walk from the Regional University campus.

VIGNETTE TWO

The next day, Sandra joined two other students she recognized from her class, Ashley and Monica. Together they walked to the small-group meeting of all those who would be doing their first field experience together in a literacy project at the community center of the Park Haven housing development. Once in the classroom, Mr. DuBose, the group leader, explained once again why they were fulfilling their first field experience requirement in a community setting, as opposed to a school setting. This group was to meet weekly for "training" on how to carry out the Reading Circle activity when working with children in the community center. The faculty liaison would convene weekly sessions to meet with the candidates and monitor their developing practice.

Mr. DuBose begins with an explanation of the reading circle:

> The focus of your activity in this first field experience is literacy development. You will be working with young children through a structured activity we are calling a Reading Circle. It is the name for the instructional activity you will be conducting with the children you will work with when you go out to the community sites.
>
> The whole purpose is to get the children excited about, engaged with, and participating in the act of reading. Your primary task is to get the children to really enjoy the experience of reading and to appreciate stories. This means that you will need to be animated, warm, and engaging as you read.
>
> If you consider the literacy benefits that many children from middle-class backgrounds often receive from parents who read to them often, you will have a sense of what we're trying to do with the Reading Circle. Your task is, in a sense, to provide the lap-reading or bedtime story reading that many children in these sites may have experienced much less often. The importance of this Reading Circle activity is that you read aloud to children in ways that establish intimacy—both with you and with books.
>
> Actually, children will establish their intimacy with, and connection to, stories *through* their intimacy with *you*. They get enthused about stories because they see you enthused. Children want to hear your animated voices, feel your presence as performers, and learn what you know as you bring your adult knowledge to bear on interpreting the story. Children need you to bring the literature to life. Many students in urban settings have not experienced this prior-to-school literacy connection—such as bedtime stories and other family-based literacy events. The children's literature for this activity has been carefully selected so as to promote this aim of enthusiasm for, and connection to, reading stories.

As he distributed the packets of books, Mr. DuBose asked how many had had the books read to them when they were small children. He was trying to get a sense of how many of the freshmen recalled their childhood experiences with certain books. Almost the entire group remembered the book *Good Night Moon*.

Sandra realized that it was because she wanted to be a psychology major that she was really "getting into" the discussion of the book and why it is so engaging to children. Mr. DuBose explained that going to bed has a special significance to young children. He asked them to reflect for a moment about why children are so reluctant to go to bed. After several responses, Mr. DuBose explained that the reticence is not simply a matter of not wanting to miss anything the adults do, but is also based on deep-seated fears and concerns. For young children, sleep is associated with death, with separation, and with the threat of loss.

The candidates made their own observations about the reasons *Good Night Moon* is so engaging to children and serves so well in addressing children's concerns about death and separation. Sandra contributed to the discussion by pointing out how the book refers back to other children's literature in the form of nursery rhymes, as she had recognized pieces of "Hey Diddle Diddle" and the "Three Little Kittens." She commented on the importance of repetition and familiarity of content when children are constructing meaning. The session ended with students picking up their packets and making plans for their first visit to the community center.

The next day, Sandra, Monica, and Ashley walked to the community center together, equipped with a packet of three selections of children's literature. These were picked for their rich language, imagery, and cultural identification for the children. Because children relish the sounds, rhythms, and cadences of language, all the candidates had been asked to practice reading the stories before going out to read to the children. They were also equipped with a record sheet for keeping a running record of children's reactions (a precursor to reading assessment) and noteworthy reading behaviors. Candidates were also asked to keep track, as well as they could, of the books that were read, language varieties involved in the interactions, behaviors, and any other relevant data.

Sandra remembered how, on the previous day, Mr. DuBose had asked how many of them remembered the stories read to them as children. Although she vividly remembered *Good Night Moon* (by Margaret Wise Brown), she had never heard of *Corduroy* (by Don Freeman) and *So Much* (by Trish Cooke), the other two books in her packet. Even though she had practiced reading the books, her mind went back to the sound of Mr. DuBose's voice when he read *Good Night Moon* to the group in order to model the sort of engaging, enthusiastic reading that elicits young children's participation.

CONCLUSION

What are the requirements for effective urban teacher preparation in a community context? They correspond to the qualities of the university–community–school partnership described earlier. These include devoting at least part of the teacher improvement agenda to the creation of a new generation of *community teachers* and grounding professional teacher knowledge in successful practices, not generic standards of performance. What are the prospects for new candidates to reach across borders of race, class, and privilege to connect individually with a group of children in ways that also advance their abilities as caring professionals? Once again, the prospects lie in creating a context for the development of accomplished urban teachers. Classroom coursework devoted to teaching to diversity goes only so far. Real cultural knowledge for "multicultural competence" requires real practice and real experience in diverse settings.

The community partnership model of teacher preparation addresses both the need for greater scholastic ministry to individual students and the constraints on doing this in school settings. Even though Sandra was enthused about becoming a good reading teacher, she understood that the quality of her experience was due to her learning how to establish warm and caring connections with children. She understood that the abilities she was developing about how to establish relationships with her students would have as much significance as or more significance than what she knew about reading instruction.

This case study and those to follow illustrate a system of practice that an urban-focused, community-dedicated, and practice-oriented school of education needs for the preparation of teachers in the new national agenda. All of the *practices* illustrated in the cases are authentic and describe real occurrences. They have been rewritten as composites to make more explicit certain points and to protect anonymity.

This case study and those that follow show the nature of a successful developmental trajectory of candidates who are European American, culturally mainstream, monolingual students from middle- to upper-middle-class backgrounds. *Community teacher* connotes an accomplished practitioner in culturally, linguistically, and economically diverse urban communities. The framework posits the following operating ideas:

1. The expectation that this largely White, middle-class, monolingual, culturally mainstream corps of potential teachers will become accomplished culturally responsive teachers is not unrealistic, provided that the entire trajectory of their development and transformation is conceptualized and built into a curriculum.

2. A new notion of practice is necessary: Practice is not simply what one does but must be understood to be some commonly recognizable knowledge-in-use that produces the desired result. This notion differs slightly from some contemporary understandings of practice. Sandra is not practicing reading instruction as much as

she is entering into the practices of literacy instruction in community contexts.

3. In developing the trajectory of development in the program of study, considerable collaboration with community partners is elicited by the school of education.

4. The co-construction of new contexts for collaborative work across sites, institutions, professions, disciplines, locations, and roles is essential. As explained in Chapter 2, these new contexts are referred to as *circles of practice* and *communities of practice*. When they are small, determined by a common specific enterprise in a common space (e.g., clinical triad, grade-level teams), they are *circles of practice*. When they are larger, involving more individuals across institutions who share a number of interests, enterprises, or initiatives, they are called *communities of practice*.

The next chapter articulates the type of arrangements that school, university, and community partners need to strive for these qualities in the system for preparing community teachers.

CHAPTER 4

The Development of Practice in Community Partnership

Participation here refers not just to local events of engagement in certain activities with certain people, but to a more encompassing process of being active participants in the practices *of social communities and constructing* identities *in relation to these communities.*

—E. Wenger, 1999

THE EDUCATIONAL LITERATURE ON SCHOOL REFORM, teacher preparation, and professional development often extols the value of *collaborative work* among teachers, university educators, parents, and community stakeholders. Yet little is made of this ability as a requirement for accomplished teaching practice. This is true even though the two major professional organizations that articulate professional standards for teaching practice—the National Board for Professional Teaching Standards (NBPTS) for accomplished teachers, and the Interstate New Teacher Assessment and Support Consortium (INTASC) for beginning teachers—posit *professional and community collaboration* as a performance standard for teachers.

Despite being prominently advocated by the NBPTS and INTASC, the *ability to work collaboratively with others* is rarely found in the initial licensing requirements of teachers, as a performance requirement for preservice teacher preparation, or in the professional development of licensed teachers. According a report of the Center for Research on the Education of Students Placed at Risk (CRESPAR), not one of the 50 state departments of education in this country required a course on family and community

71

involvement for licensing (Epstein, Sanders, & Clark, 1999). Furthermore, according to the report, not one of the 50 state departments of education included the competency for "family and community involvement" in its recertification requirements.

Why is this so? Why should arguably the most important set of teacher competencies in urban education—family and community involvement—be left out of the requirements for both beginning and accomplished teachers? Perhaps part of the answer is that the means by which this competency can be assessed has not been satisfactorily developed. Neither have the standards of effective practice involving community and family been developed in systematic ways.

The gap between the importance of teacher efficacy in family and community involvement—acknowledged by schools, colleges, and departments of education (SCDE)—and the absence of this standard in the actual requirements for professional practice is an aspect of the crisis of knowledge discussed earlier. The professional setting of the urban teacher offers too few opportunities or occasions to develop this ability for productive professional collaboration. This is what makes the development of a *circle of practice*, as argued in Chapter 2, essential to realizing the national agenda of school reform through reform of teaching. The challenge for the revitalization of teaching practice in urban schools is to infuse *collaborative work* into new systems that integrate the processes of teacher training, professional development, and partnership building.

Unfortunately, school systems, for the most part, are not very successful in systematically developing the professional abilities of their teachers. This is particularly true with regard to the abilities of professional and parental collaboration—arguably the most important ability for effective work in underresourced urban public schools. In teacher preparation in general, preservice teachers may collaborate with cooperating teachers and university faculty, but only for their own training—rarely as part of an authentic agenda for school development or improvement of teaching practice overall.

Similarly, a large metropolitan school district rarely provides a systematic program for improving the practice of its faculty in a way that *assesses improvements in their practice*. Teacher assessments, if they are made at all, are too often static snapshot assessments predicated on only a handful of classroom visits by an administrator whose principal criterion is classroom decorum.

Professional development typically consists of requiring teachers to amass a certain number of professional development points or credits awarded on the basis of *participation* in events—inservices, workshops, professional conferences, and other "professional experiences." In general, there are few opportunities, settings, or requirements for educators in urban systems to develop their capacity for collaborative work or to improve their teaching practice. Further, too few demands are placed on SCDEs to require effective collaborative practice with families and communities, because the parents and community stakeholders most likely to articulate those demands are infrequently included in the partnership (Murrell, 1998).

This chapter further explains and illustrates the ideas of a *community of practice* and a *circle of practice* introduced in Chapter 2. Recall that *community of practice* was defined there as a structured context in which preservice and cooperating teachers, through common professional activity, acquire essential theory, determine core aims, and develop effective practices for building school and classroom communities. A community of practice is the working context for the type of collaborative work that INTASC, NBTPS, National Council for Accreditation of Teacher Education (NCATE), and an array of other professional organizations and agencies call for in the revision of teacher preparation.

The community of practice specifies a structured setting of deliberate, systematic, and collective professional activity devoted to improving instructional practice and achievement outcomes. Recall also from Chapter 2 the notion of a circle of practice, an enclave of educators including a teacher educator, a K–12 teacher, and others who collaborate on a wider range of professional activity than that of training a student teacher. I argued that the logical developmental progression of partnerships is the expansion of *circles of practice* into *communities of practice*.

For the conceptual framework presented in these pages, the notion of a community of practice links the growth of teachers' pedagogical ability with the academic, intellectual, and social development of diverse learners in urban schools. It also links the enterprise of teacher preparation with the ongoing development of practices in the school that elevate the academic achievement and development of learners. Finally, the community of practice links the development of professional activity in community settings to contexts other than schools, such as after-school programs.

APPRAISAL OF PRACTICE AND COLLABORATIVE WORK

Building practices for successful work with diverse learners is not simply a matter of identifying the "right" techniques and strategies. Nor is it merely a matter of installing new "curriculum content for diverse learners" or packaged programs of "teaching to diversity" in underresourced urban school settings. And it certainly is *not* the installation of a multicultural curriculum. Building practices for successful work depends on the *appraisal of practice* in the contexts of real teaching and learning and within a community of practice.

Appraisal of practice is the key principle in the entire conceptual framework for the community teacher and community partnership approach to teacher preparation described thus far. Appraisal of practice is the foundational activity for all aspects of teacher preparation and professional development, especially in instances where issues of diversity loom large in the school setting. What makes assessment of practice so central? It is because the linkage of teacher performance with student outcomes in the evaluation is the most glaring weakness in the performance-based teacher quality reform agenda. The concept of *practice* in this framework links instructional activity with learning achievement results.

I have defined *practice* as a generic system of activity that includes not only what professionals do in a given setting but also what they are disposed to do in similar settings to achieve real results. Specification of a practice in this system always involves an *assessment of professional performance*, which includes criteria requiring successful outcomes for children, professional conduct appropriate to the situational and cultural dimensions of the setting, and evidence of the stability of both teacher performances and learner outcomes over time.

As discussed earlier, this notion of practice contrasts with the contemporary notion of practice that merely connotes teaching strategies, techniques, methods, and approaches without reference to outcome. The conventional use of the term *practice* merely describes the nature of professional activity. It does not capture the critical component of teachers' professional assessment of their own activity in light of student achievement results. When a teacher designs and carries out an activity, takes account of results as measured by student achievement outcomes, and assesses performance of the activity over time, then we have an instructional *practice*.

There needs to be a unit of analysis that captures the connection of teaching activity and learning activity—and the concept of practice in this system provides that unit. The significance of the practice orientation of the framework presented here is that it provides the appropriate *unit of analysis* for developing and improving teaching and learning. The practice orientation draws on, and is an extension of, the idea of the zone of proximal development, where the entire activity setting is understood in terms of both the teacher's activity and the learner's activity.

IMPORTANCE OF A COMMUNITY OF
PRACTICE IN URBAN EDUCATION

The most important component in creating a community of practice for developing teachers (i.e., assisting and assessing their performance as teachers) is the realization that schooling is historically and culturally situated, and is continually shaped by ideas of White privilege, White supremacy, and racism. This means that it would be impossible to develop accomplished teaching practice in urban schools and communities without careful consideration of the social, political, and historical context of schooling in America, and without an understanding of the cultural underpinnings of the children we serve.

The capable teacher of African American children must be aware that there is a deep and profound violence embedded in the fabric of American popular and institutional culture that is a significant and toxic part of children's school experience. Where there is not an antiracist awareness and explicit pedagogy for working with African American children and families, there persists an insidious violence that even the most well-meaning teacher will be a participant in despite beliefs and values to the contrary.

As noted in Chapter 2, a *community of practice* is more than just a shared commitment, shared endeavors, and a shared pedagogy. Any time one is working in urban contexts with African American children, there ought to be a social justice dimension to practice which requires that practitioners be culturally and spiritually in tune with the children and families they serve. Building a learning community that promotes the moral, intellectual, and spiritual development of African American children given the inequities embedded in American popular culture would require a concerted know-how—a knowledge-in-practice, if you will—and a commitment to learning both technical and cultural knowledge.

Five working premises frame this examination of building a *community of practice* in urban schools and communities:

1. Racism is a prevalent form of violence, and the exercise of White privilege perpetuates that violence.
2. To the extent to which racism and White privilege are invisible to many White people, violence is perpetrated on Black children without the perpetrators' necessarily being knowledgeable about, or aware of, their participation in racism.
3. Racism is a system of oppression and domination based on White privilege and the ideology of White superiority. If education is to help people contest this form of violence, educators must be aware of all the ways in which the system shapes practice in the "everyday" experience of schooling.
4. By merely confronting behaviors that are deemed aggressive or violent among school-aged children, we fail to contest the violence embedded in our institutions and thereby end up offering next to nothing in the attempt to create real community.

5. It is essential to adopt a disposition of development—to see one's work as developing human potential rather than eradicating what are deemed "bad qualities" from the home and community environment.

These premises need to be the basis of a shared understanding among the participants in a community of practice. In other words, these premises should be at the heart of instructional practice for teachers working in racially, culturally, and linguistically urban communities. The following case illustrates why.

CASE THREE

I turn now to Case Three for an illustration of these principles and the development of a community of practice. This case illustrates the devastating effect on the educational opportunities of African American students when there is no *appraisal of practice* of the type advocated in this conceptual framework. The obvious problems of the school are not so much the issue as is the fact that they have persisted unabated over the course of the 5-year life span of the school. The school community had no mechanism for seeing the impacts of its bad practice on the students. It is not a crime to expose children to bad practice, but it is a crime to willfully or negligently allow its continuation.

Even when each of the three participants in the clinical triad have different perspectives on race, class, and privilege, there must at least be a disposition to interrogate those perspectives as a part of their collaborative work. A clinical triad cannot become the practice-rich community of inquiry and practice advocated by the professional development school (PDS) movement without a dedication to collective inquiry, critical interrogation, and reflective practice.

Mr. Shafinsky, the intern, and Mr. Capelletti, the cooperating teacher, were European American; Mr. DuBose, the university supervisor, was African American. Although the clinical triad of Mr. Shafinsky, Mr. Capelletti, and Mr. DuBose offered a professional setting for discussing issues of schooling, it was a difficult setting in which to discuss the issues of race posed by the five premises articulated in the last section. Mr. Shafinsky and Mr. Capelletti both grew up in suburban settings in the Northeast, and neither had prior experience working with African American children in urban communities. Mr. DuBose attended segregated schools in the South from kindergarten through his junior year in high school, and he had worked in urban school settings with African American children almost continuously since leaving college.

Philosophically, these three men shared the same views regarding the purposes of education, the importance of equal educational opportunity, and the role schools should play in building good citizens. But they differed in their perspectives as to what one should do as a practitioner to realize these values. One purpose of the community teacher framework is to suggest how the clinical triad of teacher preparation can be developed into collaboration on practice—especially regarding differences in perspectives on practice—among the college supervisor, the cooperating teacher, and the candidate. In Chapter 2 I described this type of collaborative function as a circle of practice.

Mr. DuBose visited the classroom of the biology intern from the university, Mr. Shafinsky. Mr. DuBose's problem was how to move from a clinical triad to a circle of practice so that whenever pedagogical issues arose in the school, they could be examined. Mr. Shafinsky's internship was in a pilot school whose theme was democracy and the induction of young people into civic life. The school's mission was to work with urban youth who had not tested high enough to get into one of two "exam schools" in the system that provided college preparatory programs.

Although the school had been acclaimed for its successful work with "urban students"—the school was virtually all African American—the faculty and staff struggled constantly with low morale and the student body's lack of engagement. Mr. DuBose's first experience with the issue occurred on a trip he and Mr. Zed had made to the school. The principal had invited both of them so they could get a feel for the school prior to formalizing a university–school partnership.

Mr. DuBose and Mr. Zed began their morning of classroom visits by attending the all-school "town meeting." Both men soon saw that the town meeting was not the least bit democratic and noted the difficulty the faculty was having in eliciting the civil participation of the student body. The only semblance of Roberts' Rules of Order came from the teacher directing the meeting, who was attempting to get students to use the protocol.

The all-school meeting was actually an assembly in which teachers and administrators were trying to scaffold the students' participation in democratic public talk in the manner of a true town meeting. The meeting required a public vote by the student body on an important schoolwide issue, but none of the students made a case for or against the proposal on the table. The teacher leading the meeting did his best to elicit participation on the matter at hand, but he was virtually the only one speaking. The teacher conducting the meeting, Mr. Capelletti, happened to be the cooperating teacher for the intern whose classroom Mr. DuBose was scheduled to visit after the town meeting.

Finally, Mr. Capelletti called for a voice vote on the matter at hand—whether to hold a schoolwide event—but no one spoke on the prompt "all in favor?" Then came a chorus of "nays" from half a dozen African American male students in the back of the meeting room on the prompt "all opposed?" Upon this, Mr. Capelletti said, with a single pound of his gavel, "the motion carries." Upon this there was a general uproar in the student body. Students stood up yelling things like "What *is* this?" and "Ah man, that's bullshit!" The principal stood and said, "If you cannot conduct yourselves in a civil way, then we're just going to have to dispense with these meetings."

When the audible grumbling did not abate, Mr. Capelletti and the principal asked Mr. DuBose and Mr. Zed to leave the room so that the matter could be "dealt with." Two teachers came over to usher the men out. Once outside the meeting room, Mr. Zed and Mr. DuBose looked at each other and said nothing. The two men had known each other for a long time, and each knew what the other was thinking. They could appreciate the difficult task of connecting with urban students who had been disaffected by the school system, but they could also see that the challenge was not being met.

Both men doubted that the school had the capacity to meet the challenge. Mr. Zed remarked sadly, "It's ironic, isn't it, for a school specializing in democratic civility to have this display of disempowered and undemocratic process?" The two men parted ways; Mr. Zed returned to the university and Mr. DuBose waited in the lobby for seventh period to begin, at which time he was to observe the intern. The building was quiet, since everyone was still at the town meeting. From the lobby, Mr. DuBose could hear the angry voices of teachers admonishing students.

Seventh period began 20 minutes late, and the student usher who had come to take Mr. DuBose to class apologized for the delay. As they entered the room, she also informed him that because the biology lab was being renovated, classes were to be held in a study hall room for the week. Mr. DuBose thanked her. He appreciated knowing about the room change, particularly since nothing about the room suggested science or biology instruction. The room was rectangular, with eight long tables facing the front of the room. The only other furniture was the teachers' desk, some supply cabinets on one side of the room, and a worktable on the other side, near the windows.

Mr. Shafinsky and Mr. Capelletti entered together. They both greeted Mr. DuBose and welcomed him, reiterating the reason for the room change. Mr. DuBose found a place to sit off to the side as the students began entering the room. Mr. Shafinsky was teaching the introductory biology class that day. He began the class seated on the worktable, with his palms on the table and his legs dangling. There were 12 students in the class, all of them African American with the exception of 2 White youths. Today was their first day back from their internships, and they were turning in their papers.

Mr. Shafinsky informed Mr. DuBose that they were turning in papers and discussing each other's papers using the green rubric sheet.

Mr. DuBose had not brought the usual evaluation he typically used to evaluate the performance of interns and student teachers for a couple of reasons. On the first classroom visit he typically wanted to dispense with anything that felt like a formal observation so that the candidate could feel at ease in his presence. The second and more important reason was that Mr. DuBose wanted to get a read on the school practices so as to have a context within which to interpret the individual practices of teachers and the performance of students. He decided to use a rough rubric that he and others at the university had been developing specifically for use in urban schools. They had created five standards of good urban teaching (see Figure 4.1).

Mr. DuBose decided that the most useful thing he could do for this candidate was to document his individual practice against the five standards as preliminary feedback. The first thing Mr. DuBose noted was the absence of any goal-oriented teaching. The candidate, Mr. Shafinsky, was attempting to elicit a discussion of what students had liked and not liked the previous semester. Students answered that they had liked the quizzes, labs, and reviews for the tests.

CANDIDATE: What do you guys want to get out of biology?
STUDENT ONE: I want to cut something (signifying a double meaning).
CANDIDATE: You guys want to dissect? (*pause*) What goals do you have for yourself this semester?

There was a significant pause. The students were not making eye contact. Their faces were turned everywhere except toward Mr. Shafinsky. Not getting much response, he shifted uncomfortably. Students sat limp and listless, lounging and sprawling at their desks. Mr. DuBose knew that one of the school practices involved students' setting their own learning goals, but he wondered whether it was ever appropriate to ask such questions in such a tense, unstructured setting. It seemed to him too much like, "OK, kids, what do you want to do today?!"

Mr. Shafinsky continued: "OK. These are things we should keep in mind for everybody. We are going to go over cells, we are going to go over systems of the body . . ." Mr. Shafinsky continued listing general topics that the class might address during the course of the next quarter. Transitioning into the new trimester was the only reason Mr. DuBose could think of for using 15 minutes of teacher talk with nothing to show for it. He decided to check this with the candidate later. Mr. DuBose wrote in his notes:

Engagement and participation practices. These are practices that encourage and promote the interest, engagement, and participation of students—with each other and with the learning activity. These practices aim to provide *sustained effective effort* with respect to the learning activity and *sustained interpersonal engagement* with the community of learners.

Identity development practices. These involve the practices that encourage and elicit productive self-exploration and self-definition in the context of rich, meaningful inquiry about the world. They serve the developmental task of *robust identity development.* Literature selections and topic selections related to social justice and the students' backgrounds are particularly important for the teacher.

Community integrity practices. These are the practices of organizing the intellectual and social life of a *community of learners.* They require the teacher to incorporate cultural features (e.g., fictive kinship, communicative styles) and knowledge traditions of the African American heritage.

Practices of inquiry and reappropriation. These are practices of *assessing* students' *critical thinking* and determining whether students' achievement is demonstrable in their ability to interpret, critique, analyze, and use new meanings in productive ways. These are also the practices of critically interrogating practice in light of student achievement.

Meaning-making practices. These are the practices of making *cultural models* explicit and developing *discourse practices* for engaging students in what Freire calls "reading the world."

FIGURE **4.1.** Essential Practices in a Community of Educational Practice

> It's a good *general* practice to talk with the learners about setting their own learning goals coming up in the new semester; it is bad *individual practice* to seem as though you haven't yet thought about your learning agenda and to look like you are just now soliciting suggestions for your planning from the students.

Twenty minutes into the period, Mr. Shafinsky passed out a green sheet containing a rubric and a set of criteria for the students' written projects. He instructed students to use this sheet to give each other feedback on their projects, which had just been graded and returned to them. They were to work in groups and were asked to move into teams. Few students moved when Mr. Shafinsky asked them to form groups. Mr. DuBose speculated that some of this behavior was elicited by his presence—a perfect opportunity for students to "sweat" the young teacher in the presence of an observer.

As Mr. Shafinsky waited nervously, he noticed a young woman in the front simply staring at the paper with a frown on her face. He asked her, "Does that make sense?" She shook her head "no." Mr. Shafinsky turned helplessly to Mr. Capelletti, who then gave a general explanation of the school's competency system—Mr. DuBose thought, for his benefit.

The young lady still seemed confused when Mr. Shafinsky began again, saying, "OK, let's go over this sheet." He started a round-robin reading, asking a student to read an item on the sheet, stopping them to make a comment, and picking a new student to read the next item. Half way down the sheet, he stopped calling on students and read the rest of the sheet himself. This took another 10 minutes. During the reading time, Mr. DuBose noted that few students seemed connected. He noted that Melissa had been looking at a set of snapshots for the entire time. Mr. DuBose also noted glances of ridicule from both Ned and T.J. during the "explanation" of the green sheet and Mr. Capelletti's explanation of the competencies.

The next phase of the activity was to use the green rubric sheets to evaluate submitted work. Students were to read each other's papers and give each other feedback using the sheets. Mr. DuBose made it a point to ask what the instructional goal of this activity actually was. What was the purpose of having students read each other's papers? Mr. DuBose wondered. He imagined what his response to this "activity" would have been as a student—"going over" with a classmate a paper that had been completed last semester.

T.J., one of the African American males, did nothing and simply stared straight ahead. Mr. Capelletti noticed this and took T.J. aside so that the candidate did not have to intervene. He conducted a private conference with T.J. just outside the classroom door. Mr. DuBose could not hear what they were saying, but from TJ's posture and the fact that he was sent to office, he suspected it was in regard to his behavior. Two girls in the back were talking to each other about their papers, which Mr. DuBose believed had been the instructions they were given. Nobody else in the class is doing so.

Mr. DuBose made a note to himself: "There is not much you can do as a teacher if your instructional activity seems aimless, purposeless, and meaningless to your learners."

At 2:03 Mr. Capelletti and T.J. returned to the room. Mr. Capelletti said to the class, "I am very impressed with the thoughtful comments you are giving each other." Several students rolled their eyes. Mr. Capelletti continued, "But try to stay on the positive side. Does 5 minutes seem reasonable [for finishing up]?" Nobody answered.

At 2:15 Mr. Shafinsky said, "OK, let's wrap this up. OK, I'm just looking for some overall feedback—something good about the paper you were grading, without using any names. Did anything jump out at you as something that was missing?" Some students raised their hands and responded with superficial things: "good vocabulary," "good flow." Mr. DuBose made a final confidential note: "This class would have been much different if either one of these men had one of their children sitting up in here. In fact, the disposition that 'these are my kids' would have made all the difference in the world here today." Mr. DuBose hurried to organize his notes as the students filed out of the classroom. He thought to himself, "I have seen worse, but I don't remember when."

THE COMMUNITY OF EDUCATIONAL PRACTICE FRAMEWORK

The community teacher framework represents a different orientation to practice from the one that is typically the case in most schooling situations and certainly different from the school situation depicted in Case Three. It offers a constructive lens on how this sample of urban teaching practice might be improved.

The first insight concerns the ethos of the school. The *community teacher* framework embodies a dedication to children and their development, and less of a susceptibility to what I call the entrepreneurial approach to schooling that characterizes practice in so many pilot schools. The entrepreneurial approach involves, at its best, a "we can do a better job" sensibility. At its worst, it depends too much on innovations in pedagogy and instructional technology to carry the day without devoting sufficient attention to the lives, needs, and interests of the students. This entrepreneurial mentality is behind the creation of new programs that garner resources (e.g., granted charters) primarily on the appeal of their innovation and the promise of "shaping up" underskilled urban children.

It is a wonderful idea to organize a school community on the basis of civic responsibility and democratic life—but the students in this case experienced neither. Being a community teacher means having a greater dedication to your *students* than to your school's innovation, mission, or theme. The students in this case received not only a second-rate education but also a first-rate indoctrination into *undemocratic* public life and the arbitrary exercise of power.

The community teacher would understand the significant relationship between students' experience in the town meeting and their experiences in the classroom. A single innovation or good idea does not a good school make. The framework of accomplished practice for building learning communities in economically distressed urban schools must have *development of children* as its primary aim—development of children's moral sensibilities, intellectual acumen, and courage to seek social justice so that they might contest bias in themselves and in society. These are the aims of schooling that school people, parents, and community people can readily agree on, but they frequently get lost in the formal negotiation of university–community–school partnerships.

A community of educational practice must counteract the ubiquitous violence of racism—even if this means the simple recognition that your school does little for African American or Hispanic learners. Because this violence is embedded in the very fabric of American popular and institutional culture, effective educational practice requires a careful, critical, and ongoing deconstruction of racist constructions in media, curriculum, and instructional practice. It also requires an intelligent reconstruction of human systems in school to promote achievement and development. The idea is to understand schools and classrooms as social systems with their own *ecologies*. Effective practice in university–community–school partnerships in urban communities requires a systemic understanding of the classroom and school learning community as ecosocial systems.

In the case just presented, there obviously was a lack of balance— between good ideas and effective practice, between innovation and equity, between appearance and reality. Performance assessment, portfolios, student-centered learning, and cooperative learning were all highly visible qualities in the school's documentation, brochures, and public events. Yet the experience of the Black and Hispanic students belied the "excellence in education" these practices symbolize.

The intern and the cooperating teacher clearly were not yet community teachers, but they *could be* with the development of their practice. What was missing in their practice? Many would argue that there was a cultural mismatch between these two White, culturally mainstream male teachers and the African American students from inner-city communities. But the accomplished practice principles warrant a better explanation.

CULTURALLY RESPONSIVE PEDAGOGY
EXTENDED INTO PRACTICE

Many teacher education programs seem to assume that the way to prepare teachers for work in racially, culturally, and linguistically diverse urban communities is through some form of multicultural education coursework. The all-too-common lament heard from teachers struggling with multicultural education is that they cannot possibly learn about all the cultures represented by the children in their classrooms. If this were the essence of multicultural education, it truly *would be* impossible. If the teacher's notion of culture is a collection of all the "surface structure" aspects of a culture—such as customs, certain learning styles, or certain behaviors, such as whether students look you directly in the eye or not—multicultural education would not offer much to improving practice.

However, the true aim of multicultural education and culturally relevant pedagogy is to focus on aspects of culture that matter to learning—such as language features, forms and styles of talk in writing and literature, and traditions of learning. Teachers absolutely need to know something about the deep structure of their students' culture, particularly their language. This kind of cultural knowledge forms the essence of the pedagogy that should emerge from culturally reflective practice.

Sonia Nieto (1999, 2000), who quotes from the journals of one of the teachers she works with, offers this from Lizette Roman, who provides a clear notion of what culturally responsive teaching ought to be about:

> To have knowledge of another culture does not mean to be able to repeat one or two words in a student's language, nor is it to celebrate an activity or sing a song related to their culture. To acknowledge and respect is to be able to understand and apply this knowledge to everyday classroom activities. It is to be able to make changes or modifications in one's curriculum or pedagogy when the needs of students have not been served. It is to be patient, tolerant, curious, creative, eager to learn, and most important, nonauthoritarian with students. In order to promote excellence in education, there has to be a real and honest connection between the needs and cultural values of teachers and students. This is culturally responsive education. (Quoted in Nieto, 2000, p. 180)

This statement comes pretty close to the way in which accomplished practitioners in urban contexts need to view culture in pedagogy. From the framework of culturally responsive teaching, we know that there is a lot more going on in the educational lives of children than the mere *acquisition of knowledge*. Specifically, there is, in addition, the development of *identity* and *self-agency* in the acquisition of *academic proficiency*. An important but largely ignored aspect of children's and young adult's development is the formation of identity and sense of self-agency.

The active, ongoing search for, and discovery of, one's sense of self as a learner is a primary motive for students' participation in any instructional activity. Moreover, when permitted to, children readily make legitimate pedagogical choices and, in the process, develop the *academic proficiencies* they need to satisfy their hunger to become as well as the hunger to learn. They hunger for *identity, self-agency,* and *power* as the basis for their hunger of knowledge.

This hunger, what Jaime Escalante calls *ganas,* is most often gratified when teachers skillfully arrange the community setting so that all the children find meaning, intellectual depth, and relevance to their lives. Therefore, the primary task of the accomplished teacher is to skillfully arrange the contexts in which children find meaning, intellectual value, and increasing confidence in themselves.

In Case Three neither the cooperating teacher nor the intern is operating in this fashion—but *they could be with assistance.* Assistance of practice is the engine to the improvement of teaching and learning quality in the community teacher framework, a topic that will be explored in more depth in Chapter 7. The point here is that assistance is not likely to come from Mr. DuBose alone in the limited scope of the clinical triad. It may not even be that much more likely with the involvement of Mr. Zed in a circle of practice in which all four professionals meet and collaborate about instruction at the school. The current setting at the school is not likely to change unless all collaborators realize that the current practice is insufficient and that the requirements of accomplished practice will need considerable development.

What is required for productive change? What would it take to start professional development of the teachers toward becoming community teachers? First, a blueprint is needed—hence the presentation of the community teacher framework in this volume. Next, a system of practice is needed, whereby the more knowledgeable, skilled, and effective practitioners can assist less developed practitioners. Finally, a system for creating the systems of practice is needed—specifically, creating circles of practice, communities of practice, and community partnerships. These are the components of the community teacher and community partnership framework for teacher preparation. There is another component, however, that requires further discussion—cultural context.

CONSIDERING CULTURAL CONTEXT

The failure to articulate accomplished practice for diverse urban contexts is a stumbling block for many partnerships and schools of education. There have been attempts to incorporate the INTASC performance standards into a framework of practice (e.g., Danielson, 1996). However, these fail to assist the practice of urban teachers because they omit the critical qualities of practice specific to effective work in diverse urban communities. Accom-

plished practice, especially in economically underdeveloped and culturally diverse urban communities, is not well enough articulated by these
performance-oriented lists and frameworks of indicators to inform culturally responsive practice. The INTASC and NBTPS standards must be in-
stantiated in practice, in cultural context, and in activity if they are to be
instrumental in assisting the performance of urban teachers.

Although multicultural education ought to remain a component of
preservice education, there is a still broader set of practices that undergird
successful pedagogy in diverse urban schools and communities that should
be addressed—engagement and participation, identity development, community integrity, inquiry and reappropriation, and meaning-making. These
are represented by the five smaller circles in Figure 4.2. The central circle
represents the social sphere of activity and interaction in the learning community. This corresponds exactly to what we have been calling the *circle
of practice*, as discussed in Chapter 2. Now, however, rather than merely
representing the participants and activities, there are subcircles on the circle
of practice representing the domains of pedagogical practice for the participants in instructional activity. These represent the areas of dialogue that
Mr. DuBose, Mr. Shafinsky, and Mr. Capelletti would have needed in order
to effect productive change in their practice.

The circles in Figure 4.2 represent the kinds of instructional and professional practices necessary to acquire new knowledge and skills for accomplished teaching in diverse urban settings. Tharp and Gallimore (1991)
term this an *activity setting*. Hence, a circle of practice is an activity setting
in which teachers, parents, and other adults develop the pedagogy and
programming for the school.

With the idea of an activity setting it is easier to see what was problematic in Case Three. From the very beginning the activity setting—what students and the teacher actually *do* together in the class—does not seem worth
the time. Students do not *do* biology, nor do they engage in an activity that
produces some clear advancement of their understanding or skill. They do
not even *talk* about biology—only about their own past work and not with
the teacher. The activity setting is devoid of instructional value. Why this
happens so often in inner-city schools is the subject of much theorizing.

According to the *community teacher* model, the classroom level (the
micro level of activity) represents the situational context in which the
teacher does his or her teaching and the students do their learning—the
two activities are inextricably linked. There are, or should be, some goals
or aims for this instructional activity. To be a good instructor, one should
have as a goal an achievement performance that the student is striving
for. The point between a student's beginning proficiency and that ultimate
fulfillment of the instructional aim is referred to as the zone of proximal

Figure 4.2. Basic Components of Pedagogical Practice

development. The teacher's domain of activity is those actions that promote learning and orchestrate the classroom activity. The student's domain of activity is development of knowledge and proficiencies such that
their activity is transformed by teacher guidance into a demonstration
of understanding.

From the model, we can see what needs to be improved in the teaching practice illustrated in Case Three. The value of the activity setting, and
the instructional activity in particular, should be questioned. Asking students to collaboratively assess each other's written work from a past semester is not a bad practice in general, but as a situated practice it is clear
that the setting is wrong for this to be of any value. There is no indication
that either the students or the intern regard what they are doing as a
worthwhile activity, in part because the value of the outcome is unclear.
So they give each other feedback on the order of "nice use of vocabulary"
or "nice flow," but this does not improve their paper-writing performance.

Similarly, the part of the activity involving a discussion of goals—group discussion for students, giving directions for the teacher—is not linked in any meaningful way to either the subject matter or the students' interests. The intern talks in superficial ways about a written assignment and about what they might do in biology class. The activity setting for this class was underdeveloped because it required no understanding. It sometimes takes a third person—a parent or a colleague—to play the role of a critical friend and point this out. In a circle of practice, the intern and the cooperating teacher might gain perspective on the flatness and aimlessness of their activity setting and begin to build a more meaningful instructional setting. In terms of the diagram in Figure 4.2, the accomplished teacher's action is that of providing an engaging activity that students participate in and articulating the conditions for achieving the independent performance that constitutes learning achievement.

The most significant lesson from this case is the importance of understanding that teaching and learning take place within a system. In their subsequent conversations, both Mr. Shafinsky and Mr. Capelletti demonstrated that they were well aware of the flatness of the instruction and keenly aware of how the ethos of the school set the context for that instruction. The issues in the classroom emanated from systemic dilemmas, not instructional ones. Both teachers expressed the frustration that many of us face as teachers—operating a successful classroom while at the same time struggling with flaws in the school's system of practice. Trying to impact on one while working on the other is very difficult—and it is what burns teachers out. In the language of the model, it is difficult to effect change at the micro level and meso level of an institutional structure at the same time without a systematic approach.

AN ECOLOGY OF CLASSROOM PRACTICES

Every classroom community that fully promotes the learning achievement and development of all its participants can be thought of as a balanced system, as an ecology of the five components depicted as the outer circles on the diagram in Figure 4.2. An elementary school example of accomplished practice for promoting skills for *engagement and participation* is the morning meeting. Students are encouraged to engage in public talk in ways that build practices of respectful communication with peers, democratic sensibilities of participating in a larger social setting, and negotiation of social purposes and interests. Similarly, high schools can institute and have instituted (e.g., the high schools in the Coalition for Essential Schools) a similar routine—"circle of connection"—for students.

The accomplished practice of a community teacher encourages students' participation and engagement in learning activities as well—"doing" biology, or history, or whatever the subject matter is. The success of engagement and participation is closely tied with the community teacher's capacity to elicit from students a sense of identity, a meaningful sense of self in the context of the activity and among peers engaged in the activity. High schools, by and large, struggle with the development of identity practices. There is a tension between the school's demand for conformity and the student's struggle against anonymity. As human systems, high schools rarely afford their faculty the means of developing *identity development* practices. This situation is particularly dire for African American children, since, as discussed earlier, contemporary school practices are complicit in the degradation of healthy identity development among African American children. In Case Three, we saw many factors that might contribute to students' apparent alienation and apathy.

It is helpful to look at classroom participation practices and identity practices together—two of the outer circles in Figure 4.2. Let us focus for a moment on what is important in the identity development of African American children and the teaching practices and learning experiences that bring about healthy identity development. Just as language can be thought of as possessing both surface structure and deep structure, so might culture (to use Sonia Nieto's analogy borrowed from Chomsky's notion of the surface structure and deep structure of language).

The surface structure is easily recognized in forms—such as forms of address, forms of expression, styles of talk, foods, and dress. This is exemplified in Case Three by students' numerous subtle signals of derision that both teachers were impervious to. The deep structure, on the other hand, is much less apparent and not discernible merely through observation. The ideas that constitute American ideology influence the development of children, positively and negatively, through this deep structure of culture.

MACRO-LEVEL FACTORS—RACE AND CULTURE

Racism is a good example of a system of ideas that dwells differently in the cultural deep structure of White and African American children. In order to maintain an antibias atmosphere in a classroom, "treating everyone the same" would not be enough to prevent the African American children, and other children of color, from being ravaged by the effects of racism (as the ideology of domination). Sometimes one's attempts to deal with an expression of racism at the surface level (i.e., as an apparent expression of bias) results in perpetuating it at the deeper level.

Although surface-structure racism may be generic, deep-structure racism is specific to a particular oppressed group. That is to say, although people may have general biases to most or all people of color, the experience of racism by members of the groups is always historically situated and culturally embedded. So, although both teachers in Case Three attempted to treat students fairly and displayed no racial bias whatsoever, and also understood that racial tensions in the school contributed to classroom behavior, they nonetheless were participants in unacceptably weak instructional delivery for their African American students.

Ensuring that all children participate in engaging and meaningful activity and develop healthy, robust identities requires a rather sophisticated understanding of American popular and institutional culture and their destructive influence. There are, in fact, significant cultural values embedded in the institutions of America that need to be questioned, challenged, and contested. For example, there persists an ideology of exclusion and inequality through the mythologies of "merit" and "fair competition." In school settings, this ideology makes it difficult for the Mr. Shafinskys and Mr. Capellettis to see African American students as extensions of themselves and to teach as though the students were their own children. Unless interrogated, the persistent message that shapes practice in the school is that it is a normal and natural fact of life that African American students are underachievers as evidenced by their being at the low end of the achievement gap.

Other quintessentially American cultural values inimical to African American school success, such as competition and meritocracy, are mirrored in a myriad of ways. In American education, quality or goodness is defined in terms of proportions of those who are left out. Those who go on to college or to the "choice" colleges are those who have "competed" most successfully on high-stakes standardized tests that are presumed to be "fair" and "objective." In much of America, this competition for decent schools plays out on the high school and middle school levels as well. Teachers in Case Three viewed their school as a reasonable consolation for not getting into one of the city's "exam schools." This status, unless interrogated, can have profound effects on teachers and students alike. Had the school people in Case Three interrogated their assumptions about Black achievement, it is likely that they would have formed different interpretations of the students' behavior in the classroom and in the town meeting.

In America we define success in contradistinction to the unsuccessful, and we define achievement by contrast to those who are not achieving, never really contesting the fact that these contradistinctions and contrasts are there by design. Although for decades psychometricians toyed with the notion of cultural bias and cultural fairness in testing, consumers of the "testing industry" seem purposely oblivious to the fact that bias and the "spread" between those who are in the cultural mainstream and those who are not *exist by design*. Testing is in fact designed to get a "spread"—to get difference.

Joel Spring (1990) concludes that inequality is a cultural value of those in power in American society. Jeanne Oakes (1985) and Jonathan Kozol (1991) illustrate exactly how inequality is embedded in American schooling practices and policies—and how devastating it is to African American, Latino, and other historically marginalized populations in the United States. The ways in which children from historically marginalized groups react to and struggle with this form of oppression often compounds its ultimately negative impact. Consider the work of John Ogbu (1992) and Claude Steele (1997), both of whom show adverse impacts on children who are members of historically oppressed groups in American society and public schooling. Stereotypic threat is the dysidentification that Black and Hispanic students have with testing and testing situations (Steele, 1997).

There are all vitally important features of the cultural ecology of a school community, and the pedagogy designed to elevate the education of diverse urban populations needs to be systematically rethought.

NEW PEDAGOGICAL PRACTICES NEEDED

The community teacher model advocates that university–community–school partnerships have as a core activity the development of pedagogy designed to reduce and then reverse racial vulnerability. To provide an example of the deep structures of culture that need to be consulted in developing accomplished practice, it will be necessary to focus on one group at a time. As an example, I focus on African Americans. The following premises are drawn from a theory underpinning an African-centered pedagogy (Murrell, in press). The pedagogy is based on the situated-cognition perspective, which assumes that cognition is a social and situated activity, not merely a matter of individuals' acquiring knowledge that is abstract and independent of the setting.

To ask what African-centered pedagogy is, is to ask what teaching and learning are like when they are centered in the African American cultural heritage. Learning and teaching have five distinct features when they are centered and contextualized in the African American cultural heritage. These five features form the foundations of my pedagogical theory. In the community teacher model, these are identity development, community integrity, engagement and participation, meaning-making, and inquiry and reappropriation (see Figures 4.1 and 4.2 earlier in the chapter).

These five components are adapted from Wenger's (1999) discussion of social learning theory and appropriated to what constitutes accomplished practice for African American children and youth. But similar extrapolations to Chicano, Puerto Rican, Native American, and other groups have been made based on social learning theory as articulated by Wenger and other situated-cognition theorists who locate learning in the fabric of human enterprise and the context of human relationships and activity. These theorists advocate a perspective on learning that places learning in our lived experience in the world and participation in human activity.

Learning, according to the epistemology of the African American cultural heritage, is not an *individual* activity, but an inherently *social* activity. That is, from the perspective of the African American heritage, learning is what results from the learner's facilitating interactions with caregivers and more capable adults in the cultural fabric of a significant activity. This perspective contrasts with the mainstream cultural view of learning as an individual enterprise. The predominant view in both American popular culture and educational thought is that learning results from individual mental effort and ability. Contemporary thought among American educators has, in the last few decades, come closer to recognizing the African-centered perspective—as evidenced by the now trite and overused articulation of the African proverb "It takes a village to raise a child." By and large, however, this perspective is not at all reflected in the core practices of public schooling in America.

The contrast is between the historical experience of African Americans on the one hand and what have become the core practices (cf. Elmore, 1996) of schooling in the United States on the other hand. Rather than meaning winning one's freedom, helping others to escape slavery, and uplifting the community as a whole, learning has come to mean something measured by a numerical grade-level score generated by a paper-and-pencil test. In contemporary American culture, the common view of learning is that of something that happens in school, brought about by systematic actions and practices at the direction of a teacher. In the African American cultural heritage, learning has never been simply equated to schooling and school performance. Rather, it has also referred to the total preparation of the young person's spirit, identity, character, and intellect so that he or she can participate fully in adult life.

Participation in adult life, according to the African-centered tradition, occurs when young people progressively increase their acquisition of, and involvement in, the practices of the immediate community and construct identities with respect to these practices in the process. This sense of "participation" coincides with that of the situated-cognition theorists, who view participation both as an action and as a form of belonging in a community of practice (a concept to be discussed later). The situatedness of African Americans in a cultural heritage means a deeper sense of learning than that of individuals-in-communities. On this account, learning for individuals is an issue of engaging in, and contributing to, the practices of their communities, not merely self-advancement. For communities, learning is an issue of refining practices to enable young people and ensure progress and prosperity for them in coming generations (this is also a part of the situated activity theory thinking; see Wenger, 1999, p. 7).

COMMUNITY OF PRACTICE AND CASE THREE

The high school in Case Three could move toward a community of practice with the university if it were possible to create opportunities to seriously consider the requirements of accomplished practice for the African American student body. This process might begin with the collaboration of Mr. DuBose, Mr. Shafinsky, and Mr. Capelletti, who currently compose a clinical triad. This clinical triad could be expanded into a circle of practice in which they would systematically interrogate teaching practice in light of the needs and dispositions of the students.

If there were professional spaces in which Mr. DuBose could raise his concerns about the nature of instruction, there could be a movement toward a community of practice. But as we have said, Mr. DuBose is not likely to move this agenda on his own unilaterally. There would need to be a broader context of conversation and work. For example, Mr. Zed might become involved and express the concern he has about the ethos and the practices of the school from the standpoint of the school's acceptability as a partnering institution with the university.

SUMMARY

What is required for productive change is a new system of practice that starts professional development of teachers and candidates toward becoming community teachers. This productive change has three parts. First, a blueprint is needed—and is provided by the community teacher framework. Next, a system of practice is needed, whereby more knowledgeable, skilled, and effective practitioners can assist developing practitioners. Finally, a system for creating the systems of practice is needed—specifically, creating circles of practice, communities of practice, and community partnerships. These are the components of the community teacher and community partnership framework for teacher preparation and will be developed further in the next chapter.

CHAPTER 5

The Developmental Tasks of Teachers— Developing Accomplished Practice

Working with African American children was not as much a conscious decision for me as it was a way of life. I've worked with Black children all my life. Black children were my friends. They are members of my family. The majority of my teachers were Black. Some of them lived in the same neighborhood as I did, and they knew my mother and father.

—J. E. Obidah, Because of the Kids

All my perceptions of African American students at this time were based on my assumptions about them, which came from what I had seen or heard in the media about life in the inner city and from the students' placement in these lower tracks. I assumed that these students were so-called underachievers because of their upbringing. . . . I never considered the possibility that the tracking of these students, the curriculum and grading approaches used by teachers, and the teacher-student relationship could be contributing to the "underachievement" of these students.

K. M. Teel, Because of the Kids

As mentioned in Chapter 1, the way that we prepare teachers and other school-based professionals is on the verge of radical transformation. A new national agenda of school reform, highlighted by the report of the National

Commission on Teaching and America's Future (NCTAF, 1996), places the improvement of teachers, the quality of teaching, and the professionalization of teaching at the center of school reform. This new national agenda is generally supported by professional organizations, learned societies, public and private foundations, teachers unions, and departments of education at the federal, state, and local levels.

The new agenda for school reform has sparked a multitude of initiatives concerning how teaching quality and professionalization will drive school reform. Many of these are taking place at the level of state and local school administrations. For example, a growing number of states and school districts are bypassing the traditional college-based teacher education programs with alternate-route certification programs that prepare candidates for licensure in a matter of weeks instead of years. Nearly every state has established some alternative route to teacher certification, allowing those who do not have an undergraduate education degree to enter the profession (Zernike, 2000). In addition to this, state departments of education are now required by Congress to ensure the high performance of teacher education programs in their states (the Title II "report card"). They require demonstrations of successful performance both for preservice teacher credentialing and for the practice of certified teachers. Finally, several states, such as Connecticut and Kentucky, have standards boards that set the performance standards for professional education programs in the state.

Clearly, there will be an ever-increasing demand for demonstrating teaching quality that is quantifiable in terms of the performance outcomes of students. As the new national agenda focuses on the demonstration and assessment on teaching performance, it will be important to articulate what constitutes beginning, competent, and accomplished practice. As a result of this movement, a new perspective on practice has emerged. This "practice perspective" represents a movement away from the purely outcomes-based approach to teacher assessment that often consists of a litany of prescriptive competencies that read like behavioral objectives. Using a case example, this chapter illustrates this practice perspective as it identifies the developmental tasks of teachers in light of the new constraints, demands, and requirements of successful practice.

THE NOTION OF PRACTICE

The practice perspective of the community teacher model suggests a new notion of practice and proposes a system by which to specify, document, assist, and assess the development of teachers' ability to teach. What is this new practice perspective? First, the *concept of practice*—the site of teaching and learning—locates teaching performance in a particular setting and within a particular set of aims and cultural constraints. In the model, the discussion of practice always includes specific reference to the activity setting, cultural scene, and aims of the participants. The setting includes the cultural and symbolic setting in addition to the physical and organizational features of a classroom.

Second, in the community teacher model teaching practice is evaluated by *looking at the performance of teachers and learners simultaneously*. The teaching performance of a teacher can never be fully, authentically, and accurately assessed independently of the situational, cultural, and physical setting in which it occurs. As it is used here, the term *practice* connotes both the activity and outcome of instructional aims (learning) or professional aims (teaching). The outcome is articulated as both candidate performance and learner achievement. Analogous to the distinction between *instructional activity settings* and *professional activity settings* in Chapter 2, here I distinguish between *instructional practices* and *professional practices* (see Figure 5.1 for a glossary of terms).

Instructional practices constitute the core of a teacher preparation curriculum. Instructional practices include lesson planning, curriculum development, managing classrooms, and assessing learners' work. *Professional practices* are often addressed in various field components in a teacher preparation curriculum, up to and including student teaching. However, the range of professional practices extends beyond classroom instruction to include such things as parent conferences and team meetings. In addition to classroom practice, teachers must be able to institute systems of assessment, record keeping, connecting with parents, and professional development.

The *professional activities* of "system design" often require effective collaboration with colleagues. Among familiar professional practices are "classroom management," effective communication with parents about their children's academic progress, collaboration with colleagues on school-related tasks, and assessment of students' academic progress. In each instance of a practice—whether it is an instructional or a professional practice—there should always be a determination of whether student learning and personal development have resulted.

In this practice perspective, the action or activity of a teacher is not considered a practice unless a demonstrable instructional or developmental outcome occurs for the learners. This is a decidedly Vygotskian definition of practice in that *both learner performance and teacher performance determine the practice*. This framework looks at teaching practice as though it were a zone of proximal development for some specified student achievement

Activity setting. A social configuration in which particular actions and activities are expected and carried out toward mutually understood goals. In the classroom, *instructional activity settings* include lectures, labs, debates, and group discussion when the instructional goals are clear and explicit. *Professional activity settings* include curriculum meetings, team meetings, and parent conferences, again when the aims and goals are explicit.

Assessment of practice. An assessment of professional performance, which always specifies criteria for successful outcomes for clients (e.g., students, parents), specifies how the professional conduct is situationally and culturally appropriate to the setting, and indicates how stable the professional performance and student achievement are over time. For example, the reading instruction performance of a candidate conducting a reading group would need to be evaluated not only in terms of how children behaved but also in terms of how successful the candidate was in promoting documentable progress for each child.

Accomplished practice. A way of talking about the pedagogy of successful teachers that identifies the successful practice as an activity system that integrates teacher actions and student outcomes. It is a description of teaching practice in terms of the achievements of learners that result from the practice.

Circle of practice. The working collaboration among at least three types of participants—a clinical university faculty member, a K–12 teacher, and a parent, intern, or student teacher. Functionally, it is a *clinical triad* that has taken on a greater role in the development of school instructional and professional practices beyond that of simply supporting practice teaching. It is typically a working group that has included parents, community-based educators, and others engaged in the collaborative work of improving teaching and learning.

Community of practice. The next step in the development of collaborative communities after a *circle of practice.* This is a social configuration in which groups of individuals are bound together in a mutual activity with mutual exchange of ideas and values, and act toward a common purpose or set of purposes. A classic example related to cultural diversity is Uri Treisman's (1985) work with student study tables and study groups for mathematics learning.

Community teacher. A teacher who possesses contextualized knowledge of the culture, community, and identity of the children and families as the core of his or her teaching practice. In contrast to using a course-based teacher preparation curriculum, this teacher uses special knowledge that shows up as effective pedagogy and works in diverse community settings. A significant part of this context is the teacher's own cultural, political, and racial identity. These situated identities determine how central or peripheral a teacher is with respect to the core practices of a group or community.

Generative task. A learner-focused instructional activity setting. A generative task is an intellectually stimulating, culturally significant, and scholastically valuable activity or series of activities that result in the achievement of the learned performances we value most. It is the rich instructional activity (the activity that "works") resulting from the collaborative work by a circle of practice.

Practice. A situated performance that is assessed according to a predetermined standard. A practice is recognized as a pattern of professional activity or professional performance. The pattern is recognized by three things: (1) the design and enactment of professional activity; (2) the situational and cultural context of the activity; and (3) the consequential outcomes for the client.

Scripts of accomplished practice. *Activity systems* of practice employed by *accomplished teachers* that make up the repertoire of the successful teacher of African American children and other children of diverse backgrounds.

FIGURE **5.1.** Glossary of Terms for Community Teacher Framework performance, with the teacher also "moving through the zone" when the students achieve the desired learning outcome.

Teacher preparation from this practice perspective becomes a program of *assisting* and *assessing* teaching performance. The more formal, programmatic means of teacher assessment are addressed in Chapter 9. *Assistance* and *assessment* of teaching practice are the twin pillars of teacher preparation in the framework presented here. How is the development of practice organized in the program?

TEACHER PREPARATION AS THE DEVELOPMENT OF PRACTICE

I turn now to a brief description of assisting and assessing teaching performance in the development of preservice community teachers. Understanding teaching performance in terms of some unit of practice is important for moving preservice candidates from *beginning* practice to *competent developing* practice and moving novice teachers from competent practice to *accomplished* practice. In any case, it is important to understand that the quality of teaching performance is always tied to actual conditions, cultural context, and instructional outcomes. More specifically, we want to understand the quality of teaching as *accomplished practice*—sound teaching practice plus student achievement results.

- How do teachers acquire proficiencies and the knowledge-in-practice required for successful teaching of African American children in a culturally responsive manner?
- How do teachers acquire, and then use, this awareness to improve their teaching practice?
- What specific changes can teachers make in how they organize classroom life, assess learning achievement, and support learning activity that will result in quality education for African American children as well as other children from historically marginalized groups?

In the community teacher model:

Practice = Practitioner Activity + Learning Outcome

In this formulation, the practitioner's activity includes creating the conditions for learning—the instructional activity setting. An instructional practice is the specification of the pedagogical activity and the instructional outcome results in the realization of instructional or developmental aims. An instructional practice is never completely specified without the learning outcome for the learners. For example, if the teacher conducts a reading group, but none of the children participate or read, it cannot be a practice of reading instruction.

If we wanted to be more specific about the actions of the instructor, we might make a distinction between the preparation activity and the orchestration of an instructional activity setting. On this account we can view practice as incorporating preparation, orchestration of an instructional activity setting, and determination of learning outcome on the part of the learners.

Practice = Practitioner Activity + Instructional Activity Setting + Learning Outcome

According to the community teacher model there is no learning outcome unless the learner participates in the instructional activity setting. Hence practice becomes:

Practice = Practitioner Activity + Instructional Activity Setting + Learner Participation + Learning Outcome

That is, a practice is determined by a combination of the teacher's activity, the orchestration of the activity setting in which learning takes place, the participation of learners in the setting, and a demonstrable learning outcome for the participants.

CASE FOUR

Mr. DuBose was the clinical supervisor for student teachers at the Frederick Douglass Middle School. It was the beginning of the semester, and he had arranged for a "get acquainted" visit to the school. Mr. DuBose had been asked by Ms. Mercer, the cooperating teacher, to observe the class to see what might be done about three African American boys who had been giving her difficulty. Ms. Mercer was an experienced cooperating teacher, and Ms. Kay, the field director, was delighted to get her as a cooperating teacher, especially since she had recently received the "teacher of the year" award from the district. Mr. DuBose was not sure at first what to make of Ms. Mercer's request for consultation about a handful of students (all African American males) she was having difficulty with. But he took it as a positive step toward building a closer collegial collaboration around teaching and learning at the middle school.

This semester was the first time Mr. DuBose had occasion to work with Ms. Mercer in her combined seventh- and eighth-grade classroom.

Ms. Camby was the intern from the university for whom Mr. DuBose served as the clinical supervisor. Mr. DuBose decided that, eventually, he wanted all meetings about practice to be done at least as a triad and perhaps more. He realized, though, that until he normalized a routine for providing professional feedback and assistance to the cooperating teacher, involving other faculty in discussions about practice would be out of the question. At this first meeting, Mr. DuBose wanted to avoid talking individually with Ms. Mercer about her instruction, as though he were talking to her in a "supervisor" role. So in the three-way meeting, he started by eliciting Ms. Camby's thoughts on the lesson.

They had just observed Ms. Mercer teaching a lesson on poetry. She and the other humanities teacher were doing a combined language arts and history unit. Ms. Mercer was the English teacher on the team, and Ms. Douglas, who was not present that day, is the history teacher. The unit that the team had devised was on the 1930s and the Great Depression. Ms. Mercer was having them read *Roll of Thunder, Hear My Cry* by Mildred Taylor. Because several of the children had wondered why it was difficult for the Logan family to stand up to the mistreatment of Whites, Ms. Mercer had decided to try something she had experienced as a student teacher. She had distributed the lyrics and played a CD of Billie Holiday's "Strange Fruit," and then had the class discuss it as a poem:

Strange Fruit

Southern trees bear a strange fruit,
Blood on the leaves and blood at the root,
Black bodies swinging in the southern breeze,
Strange fruit hanging from the poplar trees.

Pastoral scene of the gallant South,
The bulging eyes and the twisted mouth,
Scent of magnolias, sweet and fresh,
Then the sudden smell of burning flesh.

Here is a fruit for the crows to pluck,
For the rain to gather, for the wind to suck,
For the sun to rot, for the trees to drop,
Here is a strange and bitter crop.

Ms. Mercer: Class, remember how we talked about the forms of poetry, and how lyrics are a form of poetry? Well, today I brought in a poem, a song really, that was written and performed in the time period we're studying. It was also written about something that Rachel asked about the other day. Rachel, do you remember what it was?

RACHEL: Yes, it was about why the Black people didn't do something about the bad treatment they always got from the White people.

MS. MERCER: Yes. I brought this in today (*nodding toward her CD player*) because I thought it would help us understand more about what it was that prevented people from fighting back. But I don't want us to just analyze with our thinking caps. I want you to experience the feeling and sensations that this poetry performance gives you, to see if that adds to our understanding. Now, I'm going to play it three times. The first time, I want you to notice how it makes you feel and why. After the first time through, we'll talk about what feelings the author wanted to communicate. The second time through, I'm going to let you follow along—you'll have a copy of the poem that the artist is singing as lyrics. On the second time, you are going to think about what the poem is about. Finally, after we discuss what the poem made you think and feel, we'll listen to it and read it again together as to what we learned.

Ms. Camby had no difficulty eliciting discussion after each of the three phases. In the third phase, the class discussed alternative phrasings of the poem that might have communicated more of the author's sorrow, anger, and indignation. The children had no difficulty ascertaining what the poem was about. This surprised Ms. Camby a little, because she recalled that in her experience of this activity as a preservice teacher she did not quite fully understand that the poem was about lynching until she actually saw the text of the lyrics. Overall, the discussions went well. However, the three African American boys, as they typically did, talked frequently among themselves throughout the activity.

Mr. DuBose had a few minutes alone with the student teacher, Ms. Camby, while Ms. Mercer escorted her class to lunch. When he asked her how she thought the lesson went, Ms. Camby was very upbeat and enthusiastic, saying, "I thought she did a great job of teaching the poem. It was really interesting! I think that the meaning of that particular poem really had an impact on the children and tied in well with the unit and their questions about the forms of racial oppression."

Mr. DuBose replied, "Well, 'interesting' is good. Recall how often we talked about the importance of interest and engagement. I wonder what you thought of the performance that was expected of the children. Remember also how we said that learning needs to be performance? What is the activity that has children doing engaging, intellectually enticing, authentic things that also evidence understanding?"

Ms. Camby replied, "Well, I guess there was a good discussion." Mr. DuBose asked again, "Would you be satisfied that most or any children in the class came away with a new ability or understanding from the discussion of the poem?" Ms. Camby remained silent, looking at a loss for words.

Mr. DuBose wanted to make his point about the instructional activity setting in the frame of instructing Ms. Camby, rather than critiquing the lesson. Ms. Camby did her best to reconstruct an assessment of the class from her notes. She was able to restate many of the interesting and relevant comments made by the students. As she was finishing, Ms. Mercer returned and joined them at the activity table.

He continued directing his remarks to Ms. Camby: "From my vantage point, I would be concerned that too many children in the class were left out of this inquiry. The mistaken assumption that is easy to make—and I sometimes do this, too—is taking a 'good' discussion to mean that children have *internalized something worth knowing*. Even those who were participating with good comments faded in and out of the directed discussion."

Ms. Mercer, the cooperating teacher, said, somewhat defensively, "I was just trying to give students an example of thinking through a poem."

Mr. DuBose, trying to keep the tone of instructing out of his voice, said, "I can see that. I think it was a very engaging exercise. But thinking a bit beyond today's experience, what do you think that the long-term results of 'giving that example' might be? How do you know whether the experience has made any of your students more apt to interpret poetry? Do not get me wrong. I really liked the activity setting and the demonstration of how poetry can express serious topics and hard life experiences. I also think that your conceptualization of poetry was good. But think of it in these terms—if the parents of the three students you asked me to observe were sitting in the back of the room today, do you think they would be satisfied that their children learned enough about poetry? Similarly, think of it from the perspective of the language arts curriculum coordinator—would it seem to her that, overall, you were meeting the language arts goals?"

He continued, "What is the outcome of the poetry inquiry? What are children supposed to know or be able to do as a result of what I just witnessed? What is the learning achievement that the children have moved closer to? Have they moved closer and how would that be known?"

When neither Ms. Camby nor Ms. Mercer said anything, Mr. DuBose went on, "Look, structurally and conceptually it was a good inquiry on poetry. The aspect of practice I want us to recognize is participation—that everyone needs to be brought along. The flow of the discussion is a teacher's illusion—it cannot be taken as evidence of understanding by the children, when in fact none of the children, including the regular contributors, have the entire schema. This is expected when, in fact, no child is continuously or thoroughly engaged in the inquiry."

Mr. DuBose realized that he may have been too critical in this, their first conversation about the classroom. He feared that Ms. Mercer was feeling attacked, so he decided to conclude discussion on the point about the need for learning goals to incorporate all learners. He turned to Ms. Camby and said, "Note this in your journal as the accomplished practice to work toward: *Formulate clear learning goals so that student achievement can be monitored, assessed and assisted.*"

> MR. DuBose: (*turning to the candidate*) Is a lecture or directed discussion the best approach here?
>
> Ms. CAMBY: Lecture?
>
> MR. DuBose: You think so?
>
> Ms. CAMBY: Directed discussion?
>
> MR. DuBose: Now you're just guessing. What do you need to know before you can adequately answer that question? What must you have before you can assess or decide on your approach?
>
> Ms. CAMBY: The goals?
>
> MR. DuBose: Exactly.
>
> Ms. MERCER: (*Somewhat defensively*) So you think that the lesson was too abstract for the children.
>
> MR. DuBose: Not at all. Kids can handle abstract. Especially when you provide a concrete stimulus situation to respond to as you did today. I thought that was great. Kids can handle critical inquiry, too. What matters is whether the abstractions matter to them and the inquiry is based in what they know in part— and see as valuable to know and understand. The curriculum just needs to be "where the children are"—and based on abilities to think, reason, and "read the world." Instructional events that are too teacher centered leave little room for students' developing knowledge or understanding. As interesting as either Ms. Camby or I found your discussion of the poem, there was much too great a proportion of class time dedicated to teacher talk. Not everything in the class should be signaled/initiated by teacher direction. If your goal is to have them critically interpret poetry, have *them do it* instead of *you talking about it.*
>
> Ms. MERCER: I hear what you're saying, but I'm going to get to that. I have an activity planned for that.

MR. DuBOSE: That is what I would have figured. And again, I don't mean to sound like I'm criticizing. All I'm saying is, Why wait? Why not have the learning embedded in the doing? I would recommend literary rituals—such as an author's chair or the literacy circle—that children themselves initiate, sustain, run, and monitor. I would even consider ritualizing the activity setting you provided today—having something for the children to interpret and then discuss in light of the learning goals. Purposeful activity, especially inquiry-driven activity, is very important for children of this age, especially for building community and eliciting capacity for prosocial behavior, ethical conduct, and democratic sensibilities.

MS. MERCER: (somewhat reluctantly) I see what you mean.

MR. DuBOSE: (to Ms. Camby) Please note in your journal this second accomplished practice for you to work toward: Develop the capacity to do emergent curriculum, especially to address community building among students.

MR. DuBOSE: Let's talk a bit about the students you were concerned about, since that's the main reason you wanted me to come today. It seems to me that we might be able to address their issues by looking at the entire picture of the instructional activity setting we have here. I'll bet we can see positive change by doing some simple things in the organization of activity and the orchestration of interactions in the classroom. First, I noticed that you expect students to cooperate. I'd say whatever abilities we value, let's teach for. Since cooperation, teamwork, and collaborative inquiry are important enough to employ on a regular basis, why don't we make it a point to develop these abilities, especially for the students who are not "with it"? Let's organize things to increase the likelihood that Hakim, Dashaun, and Jamaal [the three boys who had been giving Ms. Mercer trouble] will engage with the activity of learning. It is evident that these three regard the teacher as lacking authority and presence. They have no compunctions about acting out as a means of provocation or eliciting attention from you.

MS. MERCER: But I don't let them get away with anything.

MR. DuBOSE: Catching them misbehaving isn't the issue. The issue is how you can induce the comportment you want and expect. The real challenge is to provide opportunities for them to do what they need to be doing. It is a matter of shaping the behaviors and ways of being that you want to see from them, as well as from all the children. Sanctions that don't occur proximally to the misbehavior are pointless.

Ms. Mercer: But I can't let them misbehave.

Mr. DuBose: Agreed. But even sanctioning misbehavior has to be in the service of development of these young people. For example, today I saw some sanctions that were ill timed—late and not proximal to the misbehavior. When you were counting off students, you passed over Dashaun, saying something like (*looks at his notes*) "I skipped you because you were fooling around."—to which Dashaun said under his breath "Oh, wow!" and rolled his eyes. What you meant as a sanction had the opposite effect—it just provided one more occasion for Dashaun to think of you as ineffective and the class as trifling and school as trivial. Or maybe he just thought that you don't like him, and his remark was a defense mechanism.

Ms. Mercer: I do get it. You're saying that punishment is more effective if I have a system and some overall comportment goals.

Mr. DuBose: That's exactly what I'm saying. But I would quickly add that these are the sort of things teachers should assist each other in seeing in their own teaching. I'm interested in working with you to set up systems of practice where you and Ms. Camby and the other seventh- and eighth-grade teacher do this for each other, rather than have this university professor come out and do this sort of awkward pontificating I feel like I'm doing now. What I could offer is some perspectives and principles regarding the uses of punishment. For example, I would point out that your sanction is only a punishment if it reduces or eliminates the proximal behavior. On several occasions today, remarks that you intended to be punishers actually were reinforcers for attention. In truth, there are more ways of using reinforcement and structuring your instructional activity setting that you can use to eliminate the opportunities for fooling around. For instance, I would suggest not giving children the option of "keep writing or listening" when students are coming to the front to present as you were having them doing third period. You're modeling disrespect for every presenter if the children think that there are some, or any, occasions when they don't have to listen to a speaker. Everyone should listen—you don't want to communicate that yours is a classroom where people can listen only if they want to.

Ms. Mercer: I realize that was a mistake. But you have to understand that sometimes I make these in-the-moment decisions to avoid interpersonal conflicts between the students.

Mr. DuBose: I absolutely understand that, and it's something I want to be totally respectful of, particularly since I do so little teaching here. There is absolutely nothing wrong with it as long as we agree that it's important to assess our in-the-moment teaching actions according to the results.

Ms. Mercer: Is this being reflective practitioner (*smiling*)?

Mr. DuBose: Yes, it is (*smiling back to acknowledge the inside joke regarding the ubiquity of term*). As for conflicts between the students, I think that you perhaps would prefer the role of a teacher who creates the social environment where children learn the tools of negotiation and cooperation, rather than being the watchdog of impending conflict. These three are old enough to take on a greater responsibility for their conduct, and they should be learning to negotiate and work through their issues. Here's an example of how merely enforcing the classroom rules of conduct can result in a bad ecology of relationships. Remember the dispute between Hakim and Gretchen? You sent Gretchen to the office for allegedly calling him "wide load" and "black bag." Do you really think that you needed to sanction Gretchen for breaking the name-calling rule? Hakim is much too verbally adroit and assertive to have been injured by any name calling. He can easily demolish anyone who seriously takes him on in a verbal bout of cappin' and ribbin'. So his reporting on Gretchen was not about being called a name per se, but was instead about causing some mischief at Gretchen's expense.

Ms. Mercer: Do you have any suggestions?

Mr. DuBose: Maybe what we should be looking at is the set of ethical standards in community building that extends beyond the limited "law and order" orientation (e.g., "Everybody can't go around calling people names when they're frustrated, or there would be chaos!"). Maybe we should think together about how to make it possible for the children to access, develop, and work toward higher moral/ethical standards. Children at this age are quite capable of understanding standards of ethics, especially if they are embodied in models, like "What do you think Malcolm would do?"

Ms. Mercer: I'm not quite sure what you mean by "higher standards."

MR. DuBOSE: I mean behaving according to ethical codes of conduct that have been internalized. I mean standards that go beyond the conventional morality of "obeying the rules" toward a community where Hakim looks after Gretchen's welfare and vice versa.

MS. MERCER: I don't disagree. But we have to remember that these are just seventh- and eighth-graders.

MR. DuBOSE: True. But do you remember the story of Ruby Bridges? She was the child who was the first African American to desegregate the New Orleans elementary schools. Ruby was a first-grader when she displayed exactly the kind of higher moral and ethical standards I speak of. We shouldn't sell these children short. They carry within them ethical standards that are not always apparent, even at very young ages. The context of school should be organized to bring them out.

I recommend instead working to help children see the purposes and value of deescalation and other forms of strategic interpersonal relationships in the context of ethical conduct. Seventh and eighth grade is when this sort of work must be really concentrated. If you reward Dashaun, Hakim, and Jamaal only for low-level compliance, that's all you're ever going to get from them.

MS. MERCER: This is good. I want us to talk more but (*glancing at the clock*) I have to go pick up the kids from lunch soon. Can you summarize for me the feedback you have for the class or maybe we can talk further at another time?

MR. DuBOSE: Of course. I'll also make a copy of my notes for you. Just to briefly summarize, we can build more consistency in the sanctions for the students. Don't let some children do things you won't allow others to do. I saw today that some students got away with things (e.g., leaving their group and walking around the room) that other got sanctioned for. Second, I would be more aware of my participation structures. Participation is difficult if the essence of the inquiry is all teacher talk. Also, during the time that you must talk, let them have references or something to look at: There is nothing in front of them—no model, no representation—to focus their attention and assist conceptualization. Finally, we might consider developing the instructional activity settings to include the three students who are an issue. There are far too many apparently bored and disengaged students during long inquiry. There are too many children who get left out. I noticed that you gave three books to that group. When there are four to a table and you know there are relationship conflicts (gender-related, personality-related), why give three books to a table, forcing them to determine who has to share and who gets their own book? This is a prescription for conflict and provokes unnecessary wrangling between them.

Before Ms. Mercer left, she and Mr. DuBose scheduled a time to meet again on the Friday of that same week.

SCRIPTS AND FRAMES AS DESCRIPTIONS
OF TEACHING PERFORMANCE

A useful way to talk about successful pedagogy is the idea of the *script of accomplished practice* (SOAP), to which I will return shortly. Using the idea of a *script* to talk about specific practices of individuals, we can avoid the pitfalls of research traditions that focus only on decisions and actions, not on the total impact of the teaching and learning activity. Applying the idea of a script in Case Four, we see how Mr. DuBose assists Ms. Mercer's practice (in the same way that a director assists) in the staging of teaching and learning performances in her classroom. He is not there to rewrite the script necessarily, but rather to refine its staging in collaboration with the practitioner so as to include the three students who were nonparticipants. The idea is to share the practice by having a representation that can be examined conjointly—the script of practice.

Scripts and *frames* have proven useful in cognitive psychology as ways of describing and exploring the complexity of peoples' ideas, meanings, and intentions as they are expressed in human performance. They are similarly useful for investigating practice—for investigating recurrent patterns in the ideas, meanings, and intentions of teachers in instructional and professional settings. The community teacher model extends this vocabulary of scripts and frames to more precisely specify pedagogy and practice as recognizable, recurrent patterns. With this vocabulary, it is easier to articulate patterns of interaction that teachers need for supporting human development and learning achievement.

I have appropriated the idea of the *script* from cognitive psychology and will use it to refer to a recognized pattern of action by an individual that is recognizable as a performance by others in given setting (or frame). Therefore, a script of accomplished practice indexes both the teacher's activity (e.g., leading a reading group, conducting a whole group discussion) and the students' activity (e.g., giving an oral book report, balancing an oxidation-reduction equation). I similarly have appropriated the notion of *script* from cognitive psychology to use as a way of representing the joint performances of teacher and learners in the activity of teaching and learning.

Ms. Mercer used a script of practice that she had appropriated from an activity she experienced as an undergraduate in college. She used the emotive, even shocking, aspects to elicit the interest and engagement of her students. The activity of teaching can be thought of as playing out a *teaching script,* with the teacher "writing in as many student parts" as possible.

I use the term *teaching script* for talking about the requirements for successful performance and use the notion of *frame* as a way of representing the specific settings and episodes of the teaching script—particularly interaction among teachers and learners in the conjoint activity of teaching and learning. A frame is the set of shared assumptions that participants in an interaction have about that interaction. When a teacher asks a first-grader "What time is it?" and then responds to the student's answer with "That's correct," the frame of this speech event is *an assessment of the child's ability to tell time*. If the teacher replies to the student's response with "Thank you," then the frame is *a request for information*.

In cognitive psychology, the notion of scripts also has a specialized meaning. *Scripts* are mental representations of the causally connected actions, props, and participants that are involved in common activities (Galambos, Abelson, & Black, 1986). Although technical, this definition is exactly the meaning we need to characterize the pedagogical knowledge of exemplary teachers in culturally and linguistically diverse settings.

Using the idea of the *teaching script* focuses our attention on three categories of pedagogy: (1) the particular *connected actions of teacher and learner* (e.g., directing discussions, planning instruction, giving students feedback); (2) the *props* (e.g., instructional materials, performance routines, instructional media); and (3) the *participants* (e.g., students, co-teachers, parents). More is said about teaching scripts and frames in the Chapter 7 discussion of how to assist teachers' performance. This chapter closes with a detailed explanation of *accomplished practice,* which is illustrated by Case Five in the next chapter.

ACCOMPLISHED PRACTICE

A way of talking about quality teaching and effective pedagogy is to use the term *accomplished practice,* which I have appropriated from the National Board for Teaching and Professional Standards (NBTPS). The term may be used to refer to a high level of teaching competence meriting the status of master teacher. In short, accomplished practice denotes the effective pedagogy of an accomplished teacher. The following points further specify what is meant by *accomplished practice*.

- Accomplished practice is determined by demonstrable (shown by tangible evidence) learning achievement and personal development for all the students that the teacher has been working with over a period of time. The NBPTS has a performance assessment system, including a portfolio of teaching that documents accomplished practice.
- Hence, any description of accomplished practice is time-sensitive, situation-specific, and based on evidence. (It is incumbent upon teacher education programs to specify the types of evidence it uses to determine quality of practice through performance. This is called an assessment plan and is required for National Council for Accreditation of Teacher Education (NCATE) accreditation under the new standards.)
- Accomplished practice is the objective of candidates and teachers seeking to move beyond the minimal criteria for licensure. The minimal criteria for licensure are described in the community teacher framework as *competent practice*; and the criteria for the lead teacher characterize *accomplished practice*.
- Accomplished practice should be specified in the assessment plans of teacher preparation programs by the highest indicators on the performance *standards*. Ideally, the same *standards*—but different levels of the same criteria—should be used to indicate the trajectory of development from *beginning* to *competent* practice, and from *competent* to *accomplished practice*.
- Program standards should be used to determine, describe, and evaluate practice according to a given teacher education program's criteria of competent practice and accomplished practice.
- The novice and the accomplished teacher's practice can be described by different criteria (indicators or rubrics) on the program standards, with the accomplished teacher's practice indicated by higher placement on the indicators or rubric (the accomplished teacher's practice has higher criteria for performance).
- Using the same standards to articulate teaching quality is important and necessary for working with beginning and accomplished teachers in partnership settings. The continuity of standards from beginning to experienced practice is what makes school–university partnerships valuable as locations for developing practice.
- Descriptions of accomplished practice are descriptions of performance-based *indicators* or *criteria*. *Performance assessment* is therefore centrally

important to determination, assessment, and evaluation of accomplished practice.

- Accomplished practice is a level of practice requiring more rigorous indicators for teaching performance than developing practice or beginning practice. Accomplished practice is the highest standard of performance.
- The program standards of performance are provided by indicators that a unit develops for a given teaching performance—for example, design of curricula, instructional management, or communication with parents. When *indicators* are used to make judgments about the quality of teaching, they are called *criteria*.
- The description of performance should always include a characterization of both the pedagogical aims of the teacher and the learning outcomes of the students. Thus descriptions of accomplished practice actually address both teacher performance and student performance.
- The description of the accomplished practice of a teacher should contain a level indicator for all the standards the unit requires. For example, if a program has five standards, then the description of practice for that candidate should include a "rating" for each of the five standards for the candidate's teaching performance.

TEACHING SCRIPTS AS A MEANS OF INTERPRETING PEDAGOGY

Now that I have invoked the *teaching script* as a conceptual tool for systematically analyzing pedagogy, I now turn to the *scripts of accomplished practice* that characterize effective teaching and learning in diverse urban contexts. These terms—*teaching scripts* and *scripts of accomplished practice*— are not introduced merely for the sake of creating new terminology. It is, rather, an attempt to build a useful and functional vocabulary for talking and thinking about pedagogy (see Chapter 6) in ways that draw on useful theory (see Chapters 7and 8). I use them to refer to assessment of pedagogical actions, interactions, and settings that are recognizable as good teaching (see Chapter 9).

There is a general script of accomplished practice that is largely manufactured by the process of developing these high-stakes performance assessments as developed by the NBTPS and the Interstate New Teacher Assessment and Support Consortium. This in itself is not a bad thing. But the extent to which the emblem of accomplished practice is inconsistent with true accomplished practice in diverse settings *is* a serious problem that has not yet been adequately addressed. The problems this causes for high-stakes teacher assessment is the subject of another discussion (Murrell, in press).

SUMMARY

This chapter has explained scripts of accomplished practice for articulating and understanding the practices of exemplary teachers in diverse urban settings. Note that this notion is not merely a taxonomy or list of specific actions associated with good practice, but an attempt to capture culturally situated practice. A case example illustrating this was presented as Case Four.

The script for accomplished practice from the mainstream cultural perspective can be elaborated to reflect accomplished practice among diverse urban populations, provided that the teacher develops the cultural competency required. Ms. Mercer's script of practice, for example, can be elaborated so as to be effective with all her students, including the three African American children she sought advice about. In this comparative illustration, the distinctions were not of generic "good" and "bad" practice. Rather, it was a matter of pedagogical style that is culturally pertinent and situationally appropriate—and that makes a big difference in the response of African American children.

This distinction would help explain how the White "teacher of the year" could improve on her competent practice to make it accomplished practice in the seventh- and eighth-grade classroom she was assigned in the all-Black school. The *teaching script* was to arrange an experience (the Billie Holiday song "Strange Fruit") as a stimulus event that required students to use the knowledge and skills that the teacher was aiming for them to acquire. "Sharing the script" through a collegial conversation on its effectiveness permitted an interrogation of why some of the African American students responded (or, rather, failed to respond) to the activity in the manner that the teacher expected. The systematic sharing of practice in circles of practice is examined in the next chapter.

CHAPTER 6

Circles of Practice— The Cultural Context for Improving Teaching

Working closely for three years with social studies teachers was the most potent episode of my professional life. On one hand, I was intellectually challenged to figure out what curriculum analysis ought to be. . . . At the same time I was intellectually stimulated, I was also pressed on a daily basis to deal with how classroom teachers view curriculum and instruction issues, and I had to operate on their turn rather than in the university classroom.
—A. R. Tom, Redesigning Teacher Education

WITHOUT SPECIFICALLY USING THE TERM *circle of practice*, the educational reform literature advocating such things as professional development schools (PDSs) and centers of pedagogy espouses the importance of effective interinstitutional and interprofessional collaboration in the renewal of schools. The idea is a sound one—that the joint aims of improving schools and improving the quality of teaching require a new arrangement of professional cooperation that disrupts the traditional roles and creates new ones—that is, new circles of practitioners from K–12 settings and university settings. For this reason, PDSs have been proclaimed as "a special case of school restructuring" in which there is simultaneous and mutual redevelopment of K–12 schools and the teacher education programs they partner with (Darling-Hammond, 1994). However, it is in specifying these new systems of "mutual renewal" and enacting these new circles of practice that the PDS movement suffers its most glaring shortcoming (Murrell,

1998). Elsewhere, I have articulated this glaring shortcoming of school–university partnerships as a problem of the quality of collaboration with a wider array of people in community settings (Murrell, 1998; Murrell & Borunda, 1998).

The importance of understanding the *cultures* in which teaching and learning practices occur has long been noted (e.g., Sarason, 1971; Sizer, 1992). As an alternative to PDS types of partnerships that fail to generate systems for successfully addressing deeper issues of effective practice in diverse settings, I propose the community teacher (CT) framework. The CT framework views program improvement as the transformation of current *circles of practice* into *communities of practice*.

The CT framework argues for the development of collaborative work in which the contexts of inquiry, teacher training, and improvement of practice can take place in the same activity location as a community of practice. Recall that the term *circle of practice* denotes the arrangement of collaborative interaction among educators in community, university, and school settings, who come together to dedicate their efforts to an activity, or set of activities, to improve education. Although everyone would agree that collaboration about practice is desirable, there are few successful models for how to bring this about consistently and reliably in large metropolitan school systems.

EFFECTIVE COLLABORATION AS CREATING
COMMUNITIES OF PRACTICE

The CT framework frames the challenge as how to move our current systems toward greater collaboration to generate communities of inquiry and practice—how to transform *circles of practice* into *communities of practice*. When university–school–community partnerships develop, what is happening is the transformation of an array of circles of practice into a community of practice in the sense articulated by Jean Lave (1988). Recall that the term *community of practice* denotes a new culture of sorts—with the institution of new practices, tools, meanings, relationships, language, and symbol structures. Wenger (1999) associates *practice* with *community* through three dimensions: (1) mutual engagement, (2) a joint productive enterprise, and (3) a shared repertoire. For Wenger, these constitute the three dimensions of a community of practice, but his formulation also provides the basis for the key distinction between a *circle of practice* and *a community of practice*—the formation of participant identity. A working group in a school can be engaged in a joint enterprise—be mutually engaged and share a repertoire of knowledge, skills, and strategies—and still not be a community of practice. An additional critical consideration is the *culture* of that group and how the *identities* of each member are negotiated in that culture.

Let me give an example of the transition from a circle to a community of practice. Suppose that a working group—a literacy curriculum committee at an elementary school—is assembled in the context of a school–university partnership. The principal and the university liaison were careful to ensure parent participation in the group by inviting parents to join and scheduling meeting times convenient for their attendance. The circle of practice here is the development of the literacy curriculum, but, as often happens, the parents are there mainly to "represent" parents, not actually to participate in the same capacities as the teachers do—as the curriculum developers.

The parents placed on, and invited to, the committee construct the identity of "only a parent." This is evident in their discourse and contributions to the conversation, as when they preface their remarks by saying such things as "I'm not the expert here, but . . ." or "I'm only a parent, but. . . ." In a *circle of practice*, this role constraint persists, and this is what distinguishes it from *a community of practice*. People's actions will be constrained and determined by the role of "parent" as long as no provisions are made from them to appropriate new identities in the setting of the group's work. At various points in a discussion on curriculum, a person with a "parent identity" might even limit his or her own participation by self-editing before even speaking—"Can I say such and such? I'm just a parent."

The important point here is that it is not only the curriculum content that is being negotiated here but also the *identities* of the participants. Without a deliberate, reflective confrontation of this reality of group interaction, the traditional restrictive roles, the assumed identities, of the participants will persist. Paying attention to how members construct and negotiate identities is part of the deliberate work of building a *circle of practice* into a *community of practice*.

In a circle of practice, this role restriction can, and often does, persist until the group evolves into a community. Just because people from diverse walks of life have found a way to meet, talk, and work together does not mean that the results of the group's work will substantially impact the deep structure of practice. When a circle of practice—a group of individuals engaged in a conjoint purposeful task or activity—gets to the point where parents assume identities that carry no less "weight" than the teacher or university professor, then it becomes a community of practice.

CONTEXT PRACTICE: COMBINING
PRESERVICE AND INSERVICE

This chapter elaborates the ideas of the *circle of practice* and the *community of practice* for the development of accomplished practice by teachers, particularly by urban teachers and particularly for successful work in diverse settings. I am talking here about a system for the induction of new teachers, interns, and student teachers into accomplished practice where a measure of multicultural competence is paramount. I am also talking about a participation structure for parents and others interested in contributing to improved schooling—people who are vitally important members of a community of practice. Recall from Chapter 2 that the clinical triad consisting of a university supervisor, cooperating teacher, and student teacher or intern is insufficient as a collaborative to interrogate and improve schoolwide practices and professional activity. I argued that this is where the PDS model gets "stuck"—by trying to work the basic clinical triad into "communities of inquiry and practice."

A new system of practice is required that can introduce opportunities for development of, inquiry of, and practices in (multi)cultural competence. The basic relationship in a clinical triad is one of providing assistance and guidance to the novice teacher. To briefly reintroduce the idea of the circle of practice as the context for the inquiry and development of accomplished practice in diverse settings, recall from Chapter 2 that it can be thought of as an extension of the clinical triad (see Figure 2.1). Expanding the range of activities, the participants, and the critical topics related to diversity can expand the practices involved in the clinical triad so as to transform it into a *circle of practice*. When the professional activity and inquiry of the group are expanded to interested people beyond the immediate setting (the *community of practice*), it then becomes the means for a conjoint process of teacher training and professional development. In summary, the CT model advocates that the clinical triad should be developed into a circle, and a circle of practice into a community. Practice is best developed for preservice, beginning, and experienced teachers in a setting in which all three interact and collaborate on developing practice.

This chapter elaborates this *framework of practice*, using Case Five below to illustrate the nature of the development of cultural competence in this framework for accomplished practice in the immediate setting (circle of practice) and beyond (community of practice). As argued in Chapter 2, the clinical triad is *not* sufficient as an activity setting for doing the necessary inquiry and research to develop practice. There is only so much energy and time that can be expended by this three-person team in the short-term arrangement for the clinical training of an intern or student teacher.

At the end of a semester or a year, the intern or student teacher leaves, changing the nature of on-site work between the university person and the school-based practitioner, regardless of what other systems are in place. For example, when Ms. Camby completes her internship, Mr. DuBose and Ms. Mercer will no longer have the same occasions to talk about practice, unless these spaces are re-created outside of their work relationship in clinical supervision. Creating these new structures for continuing the professional conversations about practice is what transforms clinical triads into circles of practice.

Another, more significant, reason why the clinical triad and other current arrangements under a PDS model are insufficient as the basic working arrangement between participants in a school–university partnership has to do with theoretical and conceptual limitations to inquiry. How will the key practices necessary for developing a successful urban-focused, community-dedicated, and inquiry-driven partnership get inserted into teacher training and development of cultural competence? I suggested four categories of these practices in Chapter 4, which are listed in Figure 4.1 and depicted in Figure 4.2. There are many things to learn and understand about successful urban teaching that must be accessed through active inquiry and sustained practice. Where will this come from?

These theoretical and structural limitations of the clinical triad inform the construction of the *circle of practice* and the *community of practice*. Both are descriptions of enclaves of educators organized for the development of preservice training and inservice development in the *same professional setting*. The notion of a *circle of practice* (see Figure 2.2) illustrates the relationship between college and school partners that permits the development, as well as the interrogation, of practice in professional activity settings.

In the last chapter, in Case Four, we saw the beginnings of a circle of practice. As Mr. DuBose continues his planned conversations with both Ms. Mercer (the cooperating teacher) and Ms. Douglas (the history teacher in the seventh- and eighth-grade team), together with Ms. Camby (the student teacher), there are the makings of a circle of practice. As this group of educators continues to work collaboratively on the learning experiences of the seventh- and eighth-grade cohort, they gradually become a circle of practice. What follows is a case example of a circle of practice developing toward becoming a community of practice.

CASE FIVE

This case describes the formation of a community of practice formed from the collaboration of a new school of urban education, urban schools in the neighborhood surrounding the university, and community-based agencies and organizations that work with children in this neighborhood. This episode followed on the heels of the events depicted in Case One, describing the PDS relationship with the Martin Luther King Pilot School.

At about the time of the incident involving the concerns about a unit on slavery that led parents to organize against the school, the university opened a new school of education. At the urging of the dean, the provost, and the president, Regional University launched a new school of urban education. The inaugural event was a convocation to which educators, policy makers, and everyone else interested in, and dedicated to, exploring new and more effective approaches to urban education were invited. Many of the Black teachers of the Martin Luther King Pilot School, and many of the school's African American parents, attended the convocation at the invitation of the education faculty and later became active participants in the breakout discussion groups.

The event included afternoon workshops and networking sessions in addition to a dedication ceremony in the morning. One member of the university faculty, Mr. DuBose, organized a workshop on liberation pedagogy in collaboration with two directors from different community-based agencies that worked with adolescents in Roxbury in urban Boston.

Mr. Zed and Mr. DuBose also met and networked with several of the parent activists from the Martin Luther King Pilot School who had come to the session because they were intrigued by the title: Paulo Freire Meets Tupak Shakur: Liberation Pedagogy Among African American and African Caribbean Youth in Boston. Ms. Mercer, the cooperating teacher from middle school partner, and Ms. Hall, from the Martin Luther King Pilot School, also attended and expressed an interest in the prospect of forming a study group around literacy learning in the African American community.

THE SETTING

Ms. Martin, the new associate dean for community partnerships in education, had been working with the parent organizations in the neighborhood and had organized a community partnership with a housing project community center as a result of this networking with parents and agencies. The community center of the housing development (Park Haven) adjacent to the university had developed an after-school program in conjunction with a grant from a private foundation. The grant was awarded jointly to the university and the community-based center for the purpose of expanding community partnerships in the areas of education, health, and human welfare.

The grant, made to the university but administered by the center, was designed to "improve outcomes for student in the metropolitan public school districts and at the university and to restructure the preparation of teachers and the university faculty's way of interacting with community-based teaching and learning." Ms. Martin, Mr. DuBose, and Mr. Zed led the school of education's efforts to forge educational partnerships with all the community agencies that worked with children. Because the grant was designed to transform the way in which universities, schools, and health-care providers provided opportunities for community-based teaching and learning, it brought together individuals interested in community development from a variety of venues.

Project directors and agency heads began meeting with school of education faculty on a regular basis to develop opportunities for collaboration. The informal group began talking seriously about developing placements for students needing field experience. For the university, this offered the possibility of providing future teachers with richer learning opportunities than those offered in the university's already extensive program of "service learning" projects. For the community, the collaboration offered the opportunity to obtain a more dedicated, education-minded cadre of volunteers to work in its programs. In the past, community partners had been reticent about service learning arrangements with the university because of their dissatisfaction with the old "service learning" model. The complaints were that faculty involved in service learning were remote and unapproachable and that even though students did projects, they did not establish relationships or leave a worthwhile legacy at the site. Although the service learning program had created many significant connections with community agencies, both sides recognized the limitations. Both sides wanted to develop a more systematic program of immersing teacher education candidates in experiences that provided more in-depth preparation and provided better service to the children and families in the community.

In a special strategy session at the convocation, the community and university people planned a pilot of the partnership collaboration with the community center in Park Haven. This group became an informal task force on the development of self-sustaining community development initiatives. Ms. Martin invited three of the Martin Luther King parents to serve on the steering committee, and they agreed. Ms. Mercer also volunteered to be on the steering committee.

Ms. Martin organized regular meetings of this community steering committee and brought in several university faculty to form an action team for the development of a community-based field experience to accompany the "Introduction to Education" course. Establishing the community steering committee was one of the first steps that the university took toward transforming its program of practice-oriented and urban-focused teacher preparation. Under the directorship of Ms. Martin, the steering committee became a circle of practice for the simultaneous development of a program of practice-oriented urban education and a program of community-based educational programs in partnering agencies.

The participants on the university side included Mr. Zed and Ms. Kay; Ms. Ernest, the lead instructor for the "Introduction to Education" course; and Ms. Martin, the university's director of community–school partnerships. On the community side, the team included three parents from the Martin Luther King Pilot School, including Mr. Douglas, Ms. Hamilton, and Ms. Eduoard, three leaders of the King parent association. The Martin Luther King Pilot School was the neighborhood school for the Park Haven housing development. Ms. Franks, the director of Park Haven Community Center After-School Program, and two of the after-school instructors in the program also participated. Ms. Mercer, the English teacher from the middle school, and Ms. Hall from the Martin Luther King Pilot School also participated.

FIRST MEETING AS A CIRCLE OF PRACTICE

At the first formal meeting of this new group as a circle of practice, the main agenda item was to do a postmortem analysis on the pilot—a program that had involved placing 60 of the freshmen enrolled in the "Introduction to Education" course as assistant teachers in community sites. The majority of these placements had been in the Park Haven Community Center literacy learning program. The principal pilot was at the Park Haven Center, and these students were actually supervised in their teaching activity by Mr. Zed and Mr. DuBose.

Ms. Ernest, the lead instructor for the course, briefly reviewed the model for field placement for the group. She reviewed the reasons for having culturally mainstream, White college students experience education issues in a nonschool community setting. The reasoning for having students experience the community context as their first educational experience was first suggested by several of the community agency directors in earlier task-force gatherings. They had expressed the importance of the university students' learning about the interests, needs, and requirements of the largely African American, Hispanic, Afro-Caribbean, and Cape Verdean student population independently of schooling practices so that they could develop a more holistic understanding through immersion in the community.

Everyone understood the struggle these college students would have developing a community perspective, especially if their first field experience occurred in a school setting. Students placed in schools first become immersed too quickly in the traditional routines and practices of school life without first having the critical interpretative lenses with which to interrogate them. Moreover, when they are placed in schools as freshmen and sophomores, candidates are not able to participate in any but the most menial roles—such as one-on-one tutoring of students, or reading to students, or, worse, photocopying materials or grading worksheets.

The group then reviewed the organization of the "Introduction to Education" course by comparing a mid-course with an end-of-course assessment of the activities associated with the field component in which students had been placed in sites as tutors. The survey asked students three questions about how the course and field placement were going for them: What should we continue? What should we discontinue? What should we begin doing?

The student feedback was mostly positive about the community field placements. More than a third of the students stated that the field experience had convinced them that they wanted to be teachers in urban schools. They liked having speakers from the community in the lecture section of the course.

The comments of students indicated that they liked having access to the *authenticity of practice*—the fact that what they did at the sites was a real contribution, as opposed to being "busywork." Ms. Ernest noted in her analysis of the survey that almost all such comments came from students who had a parent or relative who was a teacher. Ms. Ernest reported that the students liked the idea of spending a total of 30 hours working, not just observing, in a community-based site to develop understanding of urban education from the perspective of children, families, and neighborhoods in urban settings.

The group discussed at length some of the students' remarks in the survey summary that revealed discomfort with racial and cultural differences. A few of the students remarked that they felt that the course overemphasized on race and racial issues, and were concerned that they might be judged on their inexperience with African American children. Ms. Ernest reported that the cohort discussion leaders systematically addressed these students' concerns in the discussion groups.

Ms. Eduoard and Mr. Douglas, the King parents, both cautioned that what this data meant was that there were some candidates who were not destined to become effective urban teachers. Ms. Ernest acknowledged the fact that there would always be some of these young people who should not be community teachers. She also noted that one of the purposes of the new design and community placements was to identify early those students with dispositions that might prevent them from being successful practitioners in diverse urban settings. The intent of the new assessment system was to determine this early so that it could be made a developmental priority.

As a result of this discussion, the community directors on the action team resolved to put together an orientation for students to ease their entry into new cultural communities and to reassure them that they were there to learn and gain experience (Sandra Hurley's experience, described in Case Two, was the occasion of this orientation). The group also discussed ways in which students could contribute to the evaluation process of the experience they had at the sites.

In the context of this conversation, Ms. Martin offered to send a team of community directors together with the faculty members (who were already planning to attend) to a literacy conference. She wanted to encourage scholarly and intellectual collaboration between faculty and community people. From the travel budget in the grant, she offered to send Ms. Franks, the director of Park Haven Community Center after-school program, and Ms. Lynn, who ran the literacy program at the center. These two were to be joined by Mr. DuBose and two teachers from the Martin Luther King Pilot School, whose travel was co-sponsored by the school and by the university. Ms. Hall, the young progressive second-grade teacher, and Ms. McMurphy, the experienced African American first-grade teacher, were the two teachers sent. Ms. Mercer was given a small grant from her middle school to attend.

THE PRACTICE OF THE COMMUNITY OF PRACTICE

In January 1998, the Coalition on Language Diversity in Education sponsored a national conference on language diversity and academic achievement in the education of African American students. The conference brought together national leaders in education, language, and public policy to articulate what the United States must do to meet the academic needs of African American students, as well as those of other students, with respect to language variation. The proceedings of the conference were published and detail the essential programs, policies, and research bases needed to address these needs (Adger, Christian, & Taylor, 1999).

Attending the conference together gave Mr. DuBose, Ms. Lynn, Ms. Franks, and Ms. Mercer the chance not only to gel as a group but also to amass a great deal of information useful to developing community-based literacy programs. Ms. Hall and Ms. McMurphy, who only knew Mr. DuBose as a visitor from the university, formed fast friendships with Ms. Mercer and Ms. Lynn, resulting from long discussions into the night regarding what they had seen and heard that the sessions during the day.

The group found itself strategizing and coordinating the materials they would bring back. This collection of resources formed the basis for the university–community–school design of literacy learning programs for the African American, Hispanic, Afro-Caribbean, and Cape Verdean students that made up nearly three-fourths of the public schools in the New England city where the partnering institutions were located.

The teachers in the group were particularly engaged by the many illustrations of instructional reading practices for African American children that were already accessible, such as in the work of Carrie Secret (Miner, 1998) and the materials used in the Oakland Public Schools. Secret's work illustrates the instructional practices of immersion in the language and literate traditions of African American culture. The Carrie Secret interview (Miner, 1998) became a common text for parents and community-based members. Before they left the conference, the members in the circle resolved to read a set of texts relevant to African American literacy learning and varieties of English, including works by Geneva Smitherman (1977/ 1986), John Baugh (1999), William Labov (1972), and John Rickford (1999; Rickford & Rickford, 2000) as part of their continuing work together.

DEVELOPING A SCRIPT OF PRACTICE

The literacy circle of practice consisting of the attendees—Mr. DuBose from the university, Ms. Mercer from the middle school, Ms. Franks and Ms. Lynn from Park Haven Community Center, Ms. Hall and Ms. McMurphy from the King elementary school—formed a study group on literacy development. They took on the task of developing the tasks of the university students when they arrived at the community centers. The group began by investigating what sort of literacy support young and inexperienced middle-class White students could successfully and productively provide to African American children. They attended and reported regularly at the community steering committee meetings.

The literacy group tackled the task of creating an instructional activity setting that met at least three requirements. Based on what they learned at the conference, their prime criterion was that whatever they designed should be a rich, understanding-yielding activity for children in the development of their reading, writing, and thinking ability. The group wanted to ensure that whatever was expected of children in these after-school activities also corresponded to the learning goals expected of them in their school curriculum. The group further felt that, to the extent possible, these activities should be elaborations and extensions through deeper exploration.

The second criterion the group set was that the instructional activity should afford opportunities for the adults to examine the efficacy of university students' actions in developing capacities of children, as well as opportunities to devise better practice as the situation warranted. The three center directors were adamant about wanting to have a way of assessing both the quality of delivery by the university students and the quality of learning of the students in their programs. The third criterion the group established was that the instructional activity setting and the program provide the context for agency people from the community, teachers from the school, and faculty from the university to work collaboratively on a rich learning experience. The group voted to become a formal study group that would continue working to understand literacy learning at the same time they continued their work as an action team.

THE READ-ALOUD ACTIVITY SCRIPT

By the end of the winter quarter, the literacy group wanted to present the fruits of their work to the larger community steering committee. They developed an activity script for the freshmen entering community sites as the first field component of their teacher preparation at the university. This activity script was a modification of some of the activity done in literature circles (Daniels, 1994). It was a modification of the setting that many teachers would recognize as a reading group, but with five important differences—the five practices shown in Figures 4.1 and 4.2. Student engagement and participation, identity development, deep interpretation, and collaborative meaning-making were the principal aims to be realized in the read-aloud.

The *read-aloud* activity script was designed for the instructional practice of learners as well as for use and instruction by the teacher candidates. It was designed with two aims—to create an instructional activity that would best further the dual aims of rich literacy instruction for the children, and to create an activity that would best further the aim of introducing candidates to rich and valuable educational enterprises in the community.

After the literacy group presented the script to the entire community steering committee, they opened the floor to questions. There were questions about developing the abilities of students over time. Two center directors, Ms. McAllen and Dr. Davis, recalled from prior experience that education students were much more proficient and useful in their second semester of volunteering. Mr. Zed was quick to point out that this kind of development was precisely what the new urban program wanted to capitalize on. He suggested that perhaps the group should try to articulate graded tasks or activities for the university students who were quicker studies, to both anticipate and assist the development of their abilities with children.

Mr. Zed and Mr. DuBose proposed that the script be used the following quarter for each of the after-school programs that had a literacy component. They wanted the community steering committee to regard it as a blueprint for the types of skills that would be desirable for the university students to develop as a result of their work in the community centers and after-school programs. Mr. Zed reminded the group of the reasons they had designed phase 1 of the program as they had, noting once again why it was important that candidates not begin teacher preparation by being exposed to traditional schooling routines. This was especially important because many of these practices, such as ability grouping (tracking) and behavioral management, are inimical to the academic development of African American and Hispanic students in urban school settings (Comer, 1997; Comer & Poussaint, 1992; Kunjufu, 1996; Murrell, 1993). Mr. Zed also reminded them that the principal aim of phase 1 was to get candidates thinking broadly and deeply about the broader social and cultural issues of education *before* they became immersed in the ways of schools and schooling.

COLLABORATION AS COMMUNITY OF
PRACTICE ON LITERACY

The literacy-based circle of practice and the ongoing development of a living literacy curriculum for children in after-school and community center programs thus became the joint productive activity that cemented collaborative partnership. The community steering committee approved the activity script and charged the literacy group to continue developing it. The group continued work on curriculum with university students, who were provided with activity scripts for working with the children. The group became a community of practice on literacy.

Cohort group leaders were invited to work with the university supervisor and community center staff to create an instructional activity setting that would fit the context of the beginning candidate. Simultaneously, the work of the university faculty and the center staff helped to define the parameters of beginning, competent, and accomplished practices in promoting the literacy development of children in nonschool settings.

I return to this notion of the script of accomplished practice in the next chapter. The read-aloud prepared for candidates was a script of beginning practice that allowed them to interact meaningfully, productively, and competently with children, even though they had not yet had any formal instruction on teaching reading or literacy development.

The task in scripting this read-aloud activity was to anticipate and assess the abilities of both the children and the university candidates. What candidates knew how to do partly determined what literacy learning experiences could be scripted for, and performed by, these inexperienced freshmen and sophomores who had not yet declared their intent to enter a teacher education program. The *read-aloud* was an instructional activity setting in which candidates read dramatically rich, culturally familiar, and intellectually enticing selections of children's literature to children in the selected programs.

The key point about this activity setting is that this was not the end-all and be-all of literacy instruction, but rather the beginning stage of a series of scripted activity settings through which students could develop their capacities to work with children of color in urban communities.

DEVELOPMENT OF A LITERACY LEARNING CIRCLE OF PRACTICE

The instructional activity setting that candidates began with was called the *read-aloud*. The read-aloud was just one component in the accomplished practice of literacy instruction for elementary and prekindergarten children. The read-aloud required that the college-student instructors carefully note children's reactions and interactions with the text material, and with one another, during the reading. The goal in this setting was to establish a connection—through the emotive rendering of the text or narrative that the reader provided—with the children's reflective imagination. It was an important experience for the children to have in order to appreciate the drama and meaning of the narrative.

The read-aloud and other literacy-enhancing *scripts of practice* were selected as the instructional activity for beginning candidates to help cement the core of the collaboration among university partners, community partners, and school partners. With a common focus on the development of literacy instruction for African American children, Hispanic, Afro-Caribbean, and Cape Verdean children, who made up more than 80% of the population of children, the literacy subgroup involved the entire community steering committee.

The parent council at the Martin Luther King Pilot School asked the teacher representatives to present the emerging literacy curriculum to the parents. They were interested in developing a literacy education program that parents could use with their children at home. All participants were working jointly on work they all agreed was worthwhile and valuable.

SUMMARY

We have seen in this case the emergence of a *community of practice* based in a university–community–school partnership, the emergence of *circle of practice* based on the literacy development of children in the community, and the working relationship between the two that forms a *system of practice*. The primary lesson from this case is that a system of practice must emerge from authentic work, respectful collaboration, and the humility of good anthropology in fulfilling the aims of quality urban education. This means the development of a network of practice in place of the old clinical triad model.

The conjoint development of the literacy development practice is informed by a number of questions. The general question for all participants is: What experience with literature and literacy events would be of greatest value in initiating a rich introduction to the world of books, stories, and literature for the children? The work of literacy development is enriched by the particular key questions posed from the different vantage points of the different members in the collaboration.

For the parents, the key question is: What experiences, whether in school or out of school, will enrich their children's literacy learning? For the university, the key questions are: What instructional activity setting can student volunteers run or participate in with sufficient expertise to carry it through? In what ways will the admittedly novice-level practice of candidates need to be scaffolded and supported? For the community agency, the key question is: How might the literacy learning experiences in school and home be enriched and fortified by children's activities in after school programs? The particular goals and aims of the community partners, parents, school, and school of education shape these questions.

This case illustrated how a community of practice might provide rich supportive networks for beginning teachers in a way that helps them overcome their cultural encapsulation resulting from their limited experience in diverse settings. The conjoint productive activity is the development of a *script of practice* for literacy learning and literacy teaching. The read-aloud was that activity in this case. The *read-aloud* activity script requires using an engaging, enticing selection of children's literature followed by an activity scripted to talk about and interpret meaning from it.

The university students are provided training on how to do a specialized literacy circle type of activity—the read-aloud. They prepare by reading and analyzing the content and determining what they will do for prereading, during-reading, and after-reading engagement with the children and the text. In the next chapter, I address how this beginning practice is extended throughout the entire trajectory of candidates' teacher preparation.

CHAPTER 7

Assisting the Performance of Teachers—From Competent Practice to Accomplished Practice

Learning is the engine of practice, and practice is the history of that learning.
　　　　　　　　　　　　—E. *Wenger*, Communities of Practice

THARP AND GALLIMORE HAVE POINTED OUT, from the vantage point of the last wave of educational reform, that the bottleneck of productive change is the failure to focus on instructional practice (Tharp & Gallimore, 1991). They argue that productive reform requires a new organization of professional and instructional activity in order to take full account of the social contexts in which teaching, learning, training, and professional development occur. They write:

> The major barrier to change in teaching practices is the absence of activity settings in public schools that would provide for assisted performance of those acts that must be employed in the classroom in the presence of students. Teachers, like their students, have ZPDs [zones of proximal development]; they, too, require *assisted performance*. As with students, activity settings for teachers must create opportunities for them to receive all six means of assistance. (p. 190; emphasis added)

The six means constituting a system for assisting performance are *modeling* (social learning theory), *contingency management* (behavioral learning theory), *feedback* (information-processing theory), *instructing, questioning,* and *cognitive structuring.*

As we embark on still another wave of educational reform based on standards-based accountability and performance assessment, it is startling to see how little heeded Tharp and Gallimore's message has been regarding how best to improve practice. The basic idea is that teaching practice is most effectively improved in a structured context in which individuals with different levels of expertise, and different positions with respect to children's learning, assist one another's professional performance. This aspect of assisting performance has been incorporated into the community teacher (CT) framework presented in these pages.

Since the publication of *A Nation at Risk* in the middle of the 1980s, we have witnessed a school effectiveness movement, leading into the current movement based on standards and performance-based accountability of teacher effectiveness. Despite the attention devoted to standards of performance, there still has not been a widely employed theory or model of school change that has yielded advancements in the quality of teaching in terms of *assisting* and *assessing* teaching *performance.* There is a particular dearth of performance-based systems that address effective work in diverse urban communities.

The educational reform literature does not, for the most part, deal with the specifics of actually assisting, assessing, and improving the *practice* of teachers in diverse urban contexts. The literature tends not to focus on knowledge production, especially the kind most needed—the culturally, politically, and situationally contextualized knowledge required for quality practice in diverse urban communities. As discussed in Chapter 1, teacher education is experiencing this as a crisis of knowledge. The crisis persists because too little attention is devoted to developing the *systems of practice* necessary for producing the situated knowledge needed for accomplished performance in diverse urban schools.

Although a number of policy tomes speak to the new national agenda for teacher quality (e.g., Darling-Hammond & Sykes, 1999), few specifically address the fact that most students in urban school systems are children of color and those systems are severely underresourced with respect to both material and intellectual funds. Moreover, most presume an *individualistic* notion of accomplished practice, which makes it difficult to envision systems for assisting candidates' performance through a network of experiences and accomplished practitioners.

THE PERSPECTIVE OF LEARNING FROM PRACTICE

The key to the CT practice framework is the idea that not all the requisites of accomplished practice are skills possessed by the individual teacher, but rather are embedded in the social contexts in which teachers are co-participants in practice. This argument has been supported by Cases Four and Five, which demonstrate circles of practice and communities of practice. This *practice perspective* of the CT framework is a step toward the more specific articulation of a *system of practice* for the improvement of teaching and learning. An urban-focused, community-dedicated, and practice-oriented teacher education program requires a system of practice that situates training, inquiry, and professional development *inside* the site of practice—that is, instructional and professional settings.

In previous chapters I have provided case illustrations of what the CT system of practice looks like. In this chapter, I elaborate on the CT framework to illustrate the creation of a system of practice at the program level. This illustration is set in the context of the new national agenda and its call for interinstitutional collaboration and new institutional coalitions for school renewal. The case example focuses on the reformulation of the *professional unit*, which is the National Council for Accreditation of Teacher Education's term for a professional program for preparing teachers. The design for an urban-focused and community-dedicated system of practice is predicated on the concepts of *assisted performance, accomplished practice*, and the *community teacher*. It outlines a teacher education program that synthesizes field experience and coursework into a trajectory of professional preparation. It details the necessary elements and components of a program of teacher education that anticipates and addresses the demands of the new national agenda for teacher quality.

First, however, I need to say a few things about the context of professional development, the need to develop systems of assistance, and systems of developing (multi)cultural competence.

DEVELOPMENT OF PRACTICE COMMUNITIES
IS HARD TO COME BY

In most metropolitan school systems, development of practice is done through "professional development," which to most teachers means a set of courses or discrete workshop experiences they are required to take to continue or advance their certification. Teachers are not expected to demonstrate more accomplished practice, but rather to accumulate a certain number of hours spent in inservice workshops and other "professional experiences." In short, professional development rarely elevates practice, since the professional experiences are usually one-shot, stand-alone "workshops" that rarely require a sustained effort on the part of participants.

As discussed in Chapter 2, the measure of a good inservice training is typically whether the presentation offered some technique or material that teachers could modify and use the next day for their own teaching. Contemporary approaches to professional development do not target accomplished practice. Currently, the default definitions of accomplished practice are the amorphous designations of *master teacher, mentor teacher,* or *lead teacher.* These are designations dependent less on demonstrations of teaching ability than on availability and years of service. Although it is obvious that possessing years of experience in the field is not the same thing as accomplished practice, longevity in teaching is probably the most frequently used criterion in the selection of a lead teacher or mentor teacher.

The most serious shortcoming of the conventional approach to *professional development* as the *development of practice* is its remoteness from actual teaching practice. Conventional professional development is frequently delivered independently of professional and instructional settings in schools. For example, the teaching script for introducing the power of poetry that Ms. Mercer (Case Four) used in her classroom is sufficiently unique that she is unlikely to find a professional development workshop that relates to what she did. She is unlikely to find any offering that is closely enough related to her practice to help her improve it. In any case, whatever workshop might be relevant to that particular teaching script will certainly not benefit her practice to the same degree as having a conversation with a colleague who actually observed her using the teaching script.

NEED FOR ASSISTANCE AND SUPPORT OF PRACTICE

The lack of *development of practice* in preservice programs and first-year teacher support is a long-standing and widely acknowledged problem in teacher education. The absence of a system of support and development for first-year teachers has led to sizable attrition among those entering the profession (Darling-Hammond, 1997; Lortie, 1975), not to mention the poor instruction received by the students of these struggling teachers. The solution is not only providing more "support" but also providing assistance to teaching performance. In other words, the support must consist, at least in part, of research on and development of accomplished practice.

Griffin (1999) asks a good question: Why should we take professional development seriously if it is assumed that the knowledge base for the collective professional knowledge required to teach is so meager that we expect undergraduates to acquire it on top of meeting the requirements for their liberals arts degree? He has a point. If graduating seniors have what it takes to begin teaching, how much more can there be to the profession of teaching that needs development?

Certainly, there *is* more to the profession of teaching than what college graduates bring, even if the way we currently organize the teaching profession suggests otherwise. However, is the "something more" merely the experience of successfully navigating one's first few years of teaching? I say "no." As argued earlier, accomplished practice is more than what an individual teacher knows and does in the classroom; it also involves the *productive impact* that a teacher has on the *quality of teaching and learning* in the school in general. Accomplished practice is not only individual skill but also effective collaborative work with other professionals inside *and* outside the classroom. Hence, the pragmatic questions to ask in creating a university–community–school partnership are the following:

- How can we take professional development seriously unless we first have a clear, meaningful representation of accomplished practice in urban settings to serve as a standard?
- How will we know how to organize the contexts for improving the professional practices of teachers if we do not clearly articulate what practices are worth developing?
- What accomplished practices *should be* the focus of beginning and experienced teachers alike?

Obviously, these questions have implications for teacher assessment, the curriculum of teacher preparation, certification, licensure, and accreditation—and these are addressed in Chapter 9. The focus here is on the implications for developing systems for assisting the practice of teachers and for transforming professional development. For now, let us turn to how the CT framework provides the blueprint for a closer examination of the conditions necessary to develop cultural competence in accomplished practice.

ASSISTING MULTICULTURAL COMPETENCE

The disconnection of field experience and course content is one of the most thoroughly discussed components of teacher education curricula reform (Tom, 1997; Valli et al., 1997). The major reason for this disconnect is the inability of programs to provide "multicultural competence." The CT framework employs the term *cultural competence* to emphasize the liberal arts grounding and the situated nature of the knowledge-in-practice required for effective work in diverse communities. Use of the term *cultural competence* also serves to deemphasize the tendency to regard this knowledge as a set of competencies prospective teachers are to acquire for each of a multitude of cultural/ethnic groups.

Cultural competence is similar to the notions of "ethnographic monitoring" proposed by Dell Hymes (1974) and the "humility of good anthropology" proposed by Terry Meier (1982). The knowledge base for the cultural competence of the community teacher includes dispositions regarding how one deepens shared and mutual understanding in a group composed of people from diverse cultures and backgrounds. It also includes knowing how to achieve wider and more inclusive collective practice. This inclusive membership is essential to accomplished practice because it allows cultural practices, and *cultural openness to different practices,* to become a part of the way that the group does things—asks questions, formulates problems, identifies sources of information, and sets courses of action.

The most important productive activity of a system of practice for an urban-focused, community-dedicated, and practice-oriented teacher education program is the development of cultural competence through two means. The first is integrating the practice of interns and student teachers with more experienced practitioners, so that they are prepared to teach effectively on their own. The second is the development of practice and inquiry systems in schools, so that the quality and richness of learning are evidenced through student achievement. Case One provided an example of how a school community could expand its circles of development and inquiry by including parents who were very much interested in the curriculum. In Chapter 4 I indicated five specific types of practices for cultural competence (Figures 4.1 and 4.2) that require candidates to do identity work on themselves (cf. King, 1991; Tatum, 1992) and in regard to their students (Yon, 2000). These are embedded in the program described next.

CASE SIX

CONCEPTUAL FRAMEWORK

This case is a semiautobiographical account of the process of program transformation, where an education faculty in an urban community is in the midst of "taking stock" of its programs, curricula, and urban mission. The transformation begins with an organizing question for a series of faculty retreats: What would it mean to develop an urban-focused, community-dedicated, and practice-oriented program for national accreditation? The ensuing activity and the development systems of practice are described here.

One subgroup of the faculty works on developing a statement of the professional unit's intent to develop an innovative teacher education program and is charged with producing the *conceptual framework*. They craft the beginnings of a mission statement describing the theoretical and epistemological principles for preparing teachers for effective work in urban schools and communities—to be written according to what NCATE requires of teacher preparation programs for accreditation as a *conceptual framework*.

PRINCIPLES OF THE PROFESSIONAL UNIT

The principles undergirding the education program are expressed in the belief that teaching must be dedicated to the development of learners' abilities in the context of subject-matter disciplines, domain-specific professional knowledge, and culturally rich field experience. This makes it necessary to integrate both the liberal arts and professional studies into graduation requirements.

The pedagogical portion of the program design is based on the Deweyian notion that truly worthwhile learning involves *using knowledge*—to think, critically interpret, discover, interact, and create. It is the idea that information does not become knowledge until it is used or applied. Philosophically, the professional unit is said to adhere to a belief in *praxis*—the integration of theoretical knowledge and practical understanding through a cycle of reflection, action, and critique. In this regard, the faculty members of the professional unit are Dewey pragmatists in their shared belief that learning, knowing, and understanding are inextricably linked to "doing."

As Dewey pragmatists, the faculty shares a belief that both pedagogy and inquiry *about* pedagogy ought to be based on action and reflection. This is an extension of the well-known notion of reflective practice (Dewey, 1933; Schön, 1989). This practice orientation not only incorporates action and reflection but also specifies a particular quality of reflection, discussed in Chapter 9 as *appraisal of practice*.

In this design, *assessment of practice* is the ignition key to effective, transformative teaching. Reflection is systematic self-evaluation in light of outcomes—both specific and far-ranging outcomes. These outcomes include the achievement of instructional aims in conjunction with the production of new pedagogical knowledge and new forms of cooperative interaction that develop among all participants—learners and their families, teachers, and everyone else connected with the enterprise of educating children. Such a program is grounded in experience, action, and reflective thought as the faculty endeavors to solve real problems of effective teaching in real communities.

Unit faculty members are Freirean theorists to the extent that they collectively value problem posing, problem solving, and theorizing in historical and cultural contexts and view education as action for social justice. The professional unit faculty believe that the work of preparing teachers ought to be historically, culturally, and politically contextualized as a part of critical reflection and ought to establish agency for both teachers and learners. The professional unit holds that its research, program development, and theorizing must be closely linked to the everyday practical struggles of teaching to learn and learning to teach with candidates in the program as well as with the students in the public schools with whom they partner.

As the professional unit looks to develop a distinctly urban focus, the Freirean perspective also means vigilance about the culturally mainstream perspectives of faculty and students and their tendencies toward "helperism" in relationships with school and community partners. As both Dewey pragmatists and Freirean theorists, faculty members in the professional unit hold that institutions of higher education have a responsibility to the urban communities and neighborhoods in which they are located. The broader purpose of institutions of higher education in the life of urban communities ought to be as participants in the transformation of these communities.

The professional unit faculty members are also Vygotskian epistemologists in that they view teacher preparation as developmental, interactive, and semiotic. Specifically, the professional unit is committed to a critical reexamination of the conventional approaches to teacher preparation and adopts the perspective of social learning theory. This perspective holds that the work of teacher educators is to assist teacher candidates in their acquisition of pedagogical ability, professional knowledge, and critical (cultural) perspectives for effective teaching.

The developmental perspective is represented in visualization of the program as a learning trajectory (or zone of proximal development) from beginning practice to competent practice for preservice teachers, and from competent practice to accomplished practice for postgraduate candidates. As candidates move through this trajectory, they are assessed at each of five points in the program sequence as to whether they have reached the standards of performance required to continue in the program. Figure 7.1 shows the five phases at which each of the performance standards is assessed for each candidate. Each phase has a *performance assessment* that determines entry into the next phase.

CONCEPTUALIZATION. Being able to explain and apply relevant theory in human learning, curriculum theory, cognitive development, and subject-matter knowledge; planning a conceptually coherent instructional plan; planning, successfully teaching, and self-evaluating an instructional plan; problem-solving conflicts and dilemmas in classroom contexts. Conceptualization requires integrating content knowledge with educational frameworks and a broad-based understanding of the liberal arts in order to design and implement meaningful instruction.

Phase 1 Prior to Entry	Phase 2 Beginning Practice	Phase 3 Developing Practice	Phases 4 and 5 Competent Practice
Level I. Making reasonable inferences and drawing conclusions from expository text; expository writing ability	*Level II. Applying curriculum theory, theory in human learning, theory in cognitive development, and subject-matter knowledge by planning a curriculum with appropriate assessments*	*Level III. Applying and self-evaluating one's understanding of relevant theory in authentic context—including curriculum theory, theory in cognitive development and human learning—in planning appropriate curriculum with appropriate assessments*	*Level IV. Orchestrating organic systems of teaching and learning—making critical-analytic judgments about prepared curriculum with appropriate assessments of practice*
Demonstrating command of subject areas taught, sufficient for one-on-one tutoring or small-group work in a community site	Presenting subject matter in a conceptual (meaningful) context by developing and implementing a piece of instruction	Developing instruction appropriate for context, conditions, and learner readiness	Showing a commitment to a style of thinking within one's discipline (e.g., thinking like a historian, mathematician, etc.)
Demonstrating liberal arts inquiry skills (e.g., reflection, epistemology, and inquiry): "doing history" or "doing mathematics"	Linking frameworks from: (1) content knowledge base in mathematics, language arts; (2) education frameworks (i.e., cognitive learning, human development, developmental psychology, curriculum theory)	Increasing capacity for linking frameworks from: (1) content knowledge base in mathematics, language arts; (2) education frameworks (i.e., cognitive learning, human development, developmental psychology, curriculum theory)	Showing an ability to frame student learning in terms of demonstrating understanding, not just mastery of information
Demonstrating an increasing mastery in subject-matter areas sufficient for group and whole-class instruction	Increasing mastery in presenting subject material in a meaningful context by selecting mode of instruction appropriate for the learning task	Increasing capacity to conduct informed inquiry within a discipline (e.g., how do you find things out in science?)	Modeling an adult or "expert" learning process (e.g., modeling how a mathematician "does" math, how a historian "does" history, etc.)
Increasing responsiveness to learners in a group and as individuals within the group			Assessing students' work in a way that promotes their academic development and achievement

FIGURE 7.1. Sample Layout for Performance Standard One

APPROACH TO PROGRAM DEVELOPMENT

Using the competencies from the state department of education, the Interstate New Teacher Assessment and Support Consortium (INTASC) principles, and NCATE guidelines as a framework, the professional unit has completed the task of specifying the performance standards prospective teachers need to know and be able to do as a result of successfully completing the program. The unit has adopted and appropriated the five performance standards of Alverno College (Diez, 1990; Diez & Hass, 1997; Diez, Rickards, & Lake, 1994; Murrell & Diez, 1997) and used them to create an organizational theme. The five performance standards—*conceptualization, diagnosis, coordination, communication,* and *ethical praxis*—form the strands along which the development of prospective teachers proceeds as they move through the program.

The *performance standards* the unit selected were predicated on its redesign as a community-committed, practice-oriented, urban-focused school of education. The unit has taken seriously its ongoing inquiry into what it means to prepare successful urban teachers who are culturally competent. This inquiry is based on the belief that accomplished practice means more than building up a repertoire of strategies and mastering content. Accomplished practice also requires working effectively and collaboratively with other education professionals, parents, and community constituencies. These are incorporated as indicators in the five performance standards. The performance standards and the indicators are used to articulate the professional understanding and competences to candidates.

Designing the conceptual framework also means articulating the levels of performance expected of each candidate on each of the performance standards. This is done at each phase of the program (see Figure 7.1):

Phase 1, prior to program entry, when students take "Introduction to Education" and are placed in a community setting

Phase 2, at official entry into the education program, when students take courses in human development and continue their community placement

Phase 3, when students take curriculum and assessment courses and begin their first school-based field placement

Phase 4, which includes the clinical practicum as a year-long internship

Phase 5, during which additional coursework is completed

This developmental approach involves making explicit to candidates the phases of the program and the expectations at each phase for successful completion. The sequence of phases constitutes a trajectory of development and learning throughout which the faculty is responsible for (1) articulating the knowledges, skills, and dispositions of good practice; (2) making accurate, ongoing assessment of those knowledges, skills, and dispositions; and (3) providing assistance to each candidate's teaching practice to meet standards for these knowledges, skills, and dispositions.

The professional unit's conceptual framework emphasizes *praxis*. This means that the education of candidates is not considered complete until they have demonstrated proficiency in practice. The field experience component is therefore integral to candidates' development. The expectation is that candidates should not simply learn principles and skills, but should *integrate* them with teaching practice in ways that permit them to *generate* situation-specific knowledge for effective teaching. The knowledge base for working effectively with children is, therefore, generated through *praxis*, guided by expert supervision and performance assessment, and then refined through extensive critical self-assessment.

There are a number of abilities that teachers must have to effectively teach children of culturally, ethnically, and linguistically diverse backgrounds. Among these are the ability to (1) develop an *inclusive curriculum* incorporating the intellectual, historical, and literary traditions of different cultural groups; (2) orchestrate *a community of achievement* in which every child is a full and advantaged participant in the social, intellectual, and cultural life of the classroom; and (3) coordinate an *inclusive family and community network* in which parents are invited to become extensions of the intellectual and social life of the classroom.

The professional unit encourages development of teacher candidates toward these diversity-relevant abilities through the five performance standards mentioned earlier—*conceptualization, diagnosis, coordination, communication,* and *ethical praxis.* By "performance standard," the unit means an integration of knowledge, professional skills, and professional dispositions that define what a practitioner knows, is able to do, and is disposed to do in situations requiring critical cultural awareness. The concept of development is central to the graphic outline (see Figure 7.1), which assumes that the beginning teacher will, with increased experience, refine and expand his or her pedagogical abilities.

DESCRIPTION OF PERFORMANCE STANDARDS
AND PHASES

Conceptualization is defined as the ability to integrate content knowledge with frameworks and a broadly based understanding of the liberal arts in order to plan and implement instruction. This performance standard would be demonstrated in candidates' ability, for example, to assemble a culturally responsive instructional unit from a piece of children's literature. This performance standard would also be illustrated in candidates' ability to apply knowledge of human development, literature, the humanities, and their liberal arts coursework to date.

In regard to conceptualization, candidates entering phase 1 of the program are expected to use evidence, formulate a logical argument, and make inferences from observations. However, the unit might not yet expect the level of conceptualization required for successful lesson planning or unit development at the beginning of phase 2, when candidates take a course in "Learning and the Teaching Process" and/or a course in "Human Development." It is in phase 2 that candidates independently develop instructional plans based on their knowledge of human development and their subject-matter understanding.

In phase 3, candidates are required to design effective instructional plans with appropriate integration of subject-matter knowledge and performance assessments that evaluate student achievement. In phase 4, candidates are expected to carry out their instructional plans, assessments of student achievement, and self-assessments of their practice and make necessary modifications.

Diagnosis is the second performance standard, defined as the ability to critically evaluate children's activities, actions, and behaviors—to relate observed behavior to relevant frameworks, especially in human learning and development, in order to determine and implement learning prescriptions. This involves the ability to make observations and informed inferences about student behavior and performance. Observation is an essential skill that most teacher candidates have not mastered at the beginning of their programs. Over three semesters of field work prior to the year-long internship, they spend 2 to 3 hours a week in field placements, observing teachers and students as well as working with individuals, small groups, and whole classes. For each visit, they reflect on specific questions in their field logs, a type of guided journal.

Observation is developed by having teacher candidates begin with an important instructional framework (e.g., language acquisition, varieties of English in multilingual settings) in the context of doing systematic work with children. In the first-semester placement, candidates are asked to complete a running record form for the reading performance of the child they are working with in the read-aloud activity script. These observations of children's reading performance require none of the sophistication of a true reading diagnostic of a reading teacher, but they do require candidates to develop their ability to systematically document aspects of performance. They learn to distinguish statements of observation from inferences.

In the second-semester placement, candidates are asked to *make formal observations* about the development of language and then *interpret data* in specific categories of phonology, lexicon, syntax, morphology, and discourse. Candidates have to apply their understanding of these frameworks of language acquisition and literacy learning by detailing what their observations reveal about a child's literacy development.

There are unique aspects of language, literacy, and cultural development among African American children that differ from the standard norms and expectations of White, middle-class youngsters that prospective community teachers must include in the human development component of their teacher preparation. The fact that most of the literature on human development used in teacher training is based on the culture and socialization practices of White, middle-class, mainstream norms means that candidates are not exposed to frameworks that are inclusive or representative of the experience of an increasingly diverse student population. Moreover, foundational knowledge about the cognitive, moral, and psychosocial development of, for example, African American children, distorted and degraded as it has been by decades of deficit models, is not readily available.

Preparing candidates in the performance standard of *diagnosis* requires confronting these shortcomings in the teacher knowledge base regarding human development in two ways. One of these is the fact that the foundation of human development traditionally available in teacher preparation programs, based as it is on the developmental and cultural norms of White, middle-class youngsters, is inappropriate for the assessment of low-income African American children and other children of color in diverse urban communities. The second shortcoming concerns the dearth of systematic inquiry into culturally relevant development and pedagogy.

The daunting challenge for community teachers moving through the program is twofold. First, they learn what they need to know about contemporary theory at the same time that they develop a culturally and historically informed critical perspective. Then, at the same time, they learn new theory by accessing new sources of information and by participating in the knowledge production of culturally relevant practice alongside accomplished teachers and educational researchers.

The challenge of the program is the difficult task of helping candidates to be critical consumers of contemporary theories and principles at the same time that they are developing skills of inquiry and diagnosis for accessing culturally authentic new knowledge of human development in real settings. Therefore, candidates in the program are required to develop their capacity for *diagnosis* through systematic study of linguistic–cultural knowledge about African American, African Caribbean, and Hispanic cultural/

ethnic groups (which account for 75% of the student population in urban districts).

Every candidate is placed in a field experience during the "Introduction to Education" course. When they register for the introductory course, they are automatically registered for a one-credit field, which is analogous to the labs associated with science courses. There are four such fields in the program, which increase in complexity and responsibility; the fourth field is a yearlong internship as a teacher. An example of this requirement is Sandra Hurley's legacy project, which she completed as a requirement for her "Introduction to Education" course. The legacy project was a written report with several product criteria requiring that Sandra do the following:

- Supply copies of the running record sheets for each occasion of story reading over the course of the semester.
- Provide a brief written assessment as to the reading progress of her three students, based on a review of her running record sheets.
- Write a brief self-assessment about which indicators of reading ability progress she influenced.
- Write a brief self-reflection about what she felt she had learned about the pedagogy of reading with children in the community site.
- Write a brief list of recommendations she would make to the director for how to improve both the children's learning experience and the university students' experience.

Coordination is the performance standard that requires the ability to organize and manage both material and conceptual resources effectively to support children's genuine learning achievements. The education faculty views "resources" broadly, including time, space, persons, activities, concepts, and media. A central resource for the child, and by extension for the teacher, is the child's parent(s) or guardian(s). The most obvious manifestation of this ability is in the implementation of a teaching plan. Arrangement of materials, sequencing of events, orchestration of relationships among children, and management of the activity are all part of this performance standard. Sandra Hurley demonstrated coordination in her selection of books, scheduling of reading time with her students, management of reading diagnostic records, and management of student files.

Movement through the developmental trajectory for coordination begins with candidates' capacity to make meaningful connections in their own learning experiences, as Sandra was expected to do in her legacy project. Beginning candidates struggle to coordinate the requirements to (1) develop skills, (2) master content, (3) understand concepts in deeper ways than recollection and explanation, and (4) situate themselves in actual practice in diverse urban settings. Candidates in phase 2 of the program, although in touch with what "turns them on" pedagogically, need to move to articulation and emulation of aspects of good instructional practice. The developmental accomplishment for phase 2 candidates is to move beyond "good activity" mentality—where they value and evaluate instruction according to whether it was fun and engaging for the children without critical regard for such things as whether the children learned anything lasting or worthwhile. It does seem to be an achievement for the unit's candidates to coordinate (simultaneously consider) both the engaging qualities and the pedagogical value of a piece of instruction.

Communication is defined as using verbal, nonverbal, and media modes of communication to create a classroom environment that structures and reinforces learning. This performance standard builds on the university's general educational requirements to demonstrate proficiency in reading, writing, listening, speaking, and the use of media. It also relates to conceptualization, because of candidates' need to show command of the subject matter they are teaching. This performance standard is developed across all courses, with a gradual strengthening of the various aspects of the ability, but there are educational frameworks that distinguish communication as an ability developed in the teacher education curriculum.

By far the most complex of the performance standards, *ethical praxis,* draws the other four into its meaning: acting with professional values as a situational decision maker, adapting to the changing needs of children in their social and intellectual lives, and advocacy. Although the education faculty has designed the course sequence and field experiences to build toward the ability to design effective learning experiences for a diverse student body, the most important context for developing this ability is the final field work seminar and the yearlong internship.

In the yearlong internship seminars, ethical praxis becomes the core of the development of multicultural teaching ability in the unit's program. The generativity of diversity-relevant teaching practice occurs as the education faculty draws on the experiences of teacher candidates—and the practical experiences of cooperating teachers, community partners, and parents—to inform the "wisdom of practice" component of the unit's ability-based program. In the year-long internship seminars, teacher candidates discuss issues of effective teaching practice in multicultural settings with both their university supervisors and site supervisors.

The value of bringing together cooperating teachers, community partners, and candidates in these dialogues has been important for generating practical knowledge regarding teaching in diverse settings that the department would otherwise not have access to. Discourse among teachers, education professors, and teacher candidates, from different points and perspectives, helps to particularize the abilities in real teaching contexts.

PHASE 1 OF THE PROGRAM: DEMONSTRATION OF COMPETENCY

Candidates demonstrate a baseline level of ability for each of the five standards in the community-based field placement using the literacy scripts developed in collaboration with community programs. This is called Field One. The *read-aloud* script requires selecting an engaging, enticing sample of children's literature followed by an activity scripted to talk about and interpret meaning from it. Candidates prepare by reading and analyzing the content and deciding what they will do for prereading, during-reading, and after-reading engagement with the children and the text. Candidates are asked to prepare their script for the prereading phase by thinking about the following questions:

- What is worth knowing or experiencing in this book?
- How will you get the children prepared to engage with this knowledge or experience?
- What questions should be posed? Answered?
- What predictions will be made? Confirmed?

This preparation requires *conceptualization*. When Sandra thought about these questions, she also called on her knowledge and understanding of wider issues and themes, such as what she might have learned about in her other arts and sciences coursework. In later phases of the read-aloud instructional script (during reading), the university students are further asked to think through the following questions related to *coordination*:

- How will you animate and dramatize the story?
- What props will be effective?
- What devices will you use to elicit children's participation in the telling of the narrative?

Finally, for the latter portion of the activity script, the university students are asked to think through questions that tap their ability regarding *diagnosis*:

- What will you do to highlight predictions and reinforce the story structure?
- By what means will you have the children connect their interpretation of the story with their own lives?

- How will you lead the children in an investigation of the meaning of the story to their lives and the wider world?
- What devices will you use to encourage students to share understanding, interpretations, reactions, feelings, and thoughts?

Later, in their second field experience, Field Two, the ability to interpret observational data is extended in the completion of a child study as part of the coursework related to human development and learning. Program candidates learn to compare what they see with patterns that might be expected according to theory. Through this experience, they address the issue of differences between the generalizations of a framework and the experience of individual children. They begin to develop flexibility in applying theory and a disposition to question when faced with discrepant information.

Teacher candidates progress to more complex observations and inference making in their third field placement (Field Three) because they must incorporate observational ability as part of their teaching practice. In their third field placement, candidates note aspects of their own practice in the classroom and then make inferences regarding the impact of this practice on student learning achievement. For example, they record their responses to student questions and note the pattern of student verbal and nonverbal behavior following those responses. Discovering a pattern of differential treatment of boys and girls or "majority" and "minority" students in their practice is an example of the type of development expected of candidates at this level.

Faculty assessment is critical in the development of the observational skills required in the performance standard of diagnosis. Typically, beginning candidates "mix" observation with conclusions emanating from preconceived ideas about the situation observed. Just as often, candidates may not yet know the difference between observation and inference in the early stages of their university education. The careful feedback of the education faculty assists in the development of a disposition toward careful gathering of data and toward a meta-awareness of one's own biases during observation.

The fourth field experience, the year-long internship, requires coordinating all aspects of classroom instruction—not only the necessary elements of a good instructional plan, but the material, relational, and symbolic aspects as well. What modes, media, materials, approaches, and so forth will best promote understanding of the concepts being taught? How will the sequence of steps be orchestrated, relationships negotiated, materials distributed, and resources used to bring about the desired learning outcomes? These are the questions that candidates work to answer in phase 3 of their program. Additionally, in phase 4 candidates also must demonstrate their ability to critically reflect on and assess their own practice.

In the yearlong internship, future teachers can demonstrate coordination ability by successfully handling "in-the-moment" glitches with materials (e.g., running out of solvent), timing (e.g., some groups racing ahead and becoming ready for the next instructions), relationships (e.g., "I'm not working with LaShaun anymore!"), or group management (e.g., unexpected pull-out time for key children).

PERFORMANCE ASSESSMENTS AND TEACHING PRACTICE

While the education faculty has designed the course sequence and field experiences to build toward the ability to design effective learning experiences for a diverse student body, the most important context for developing this ability is in the final field work seminar attached to methods coursework and the yearlong internship (Field Four). In both, candidates must prepare whole-class lessons. The final field is in a multicultural classroom, and one or both of the two 9-week student teaching placements is in an urban public school classroom. The metropolitan public schools have a student body composed of 75% students of color, thus also ensuring experience with diversity.

Just as the unit cannot meaningfully analyze children's cognitive functioning as separate from their culture, neither can the unit meaningfully understand teachers' ability to effectively promote learning in diverse settings apart from their practice in those settings. So, as prospective teachers, what deep learning about culture, race, and ethnicity is next? How does the unit move toward becoming more "multiculturally competent" or "cross-culturally competent" or "ethnically literate"? The means by which the unit promotes the development of integrated professional abilities is through *performance assessment.*

The program's use of performance assessment promotes an integrated professional knowledge base in three ways. First, performance assessments integrate theory and practice by requiring that candidates apply knowledge developed in classroom courses to the clinical field placements they experience concomitantly. Second, performance assessment in all cases (i.e., in both in-class and field courses) integrates the five professional abilities: *conceptualization, diagnosis, coordination, communication,* and *ethical praxis.* Finally, performance assessment requires candidates to adopt professional roles and dispositions as they perform learning tasks, so that content knowledge, skill, and professional demeanor are always integrated in the candidates' exhibition of their learning.

The program's success in helping candidates develop abilities of culturally responsive practice is due largely to performance assessment—which not only elicits the habits of mind and skills of the culturally responsive, but also clearly frames what candidates need to *reflect on*. Because performance assessment is situated in authentic contexts and teaching roles, candidates can more easily focus on specific ways in which they need to improve their teaching than they could if they merely learned about responsive teaching practice.

Performance assessment creates for future teachers an actively generative knowledge structure that includes a solid knowledge of theory and its application to practice, specific professional skills required for teaching, and specific professional dispositions. Such an integrated knowledge structure is built for future teachers through the experience of continuous evaluation of teaching performance according to criteria reflecting culturally responsive teaching. Prospective teachers learn the meaning of culturally responsive teaching not as a concept but as a set of practices. Prospective teachers' understanding of what constitutes culturally responsive teaching practice is built "from the ground up"—grounded in their on teaching performance, shaped by expert feedback, and clarified by their own critical reflection.

Times for critical self-reflection and review of teaching performance are built in at several points in the program. These are both within-course (internal assessments) and programwide (external assessments).

EXTERNAL ASSESSMENTS

The purpose of external assessments in each of the four phases is to determine where candidates are in relation to the standards regarding the abilities required to do successful work in the next phase. All candidates completing methods courses do a case study that requires them to take an original context and problem-solve in a way that reveals what they really understand about curriculum design, pedagogical theory, and learning. The assessment focuses on candidates' ability to draw on aspects of the teacher education curriculum (i.e., multicultural education principles and developmental frameworks) and to apply their abilities in *conceptualization, communication,* and *ethical praxis*.

Another example of an external assessment is the portfolio assessment, which could be a part of each phase assessment. In phase 1, the portfolio should consist of two items to be evaluated as part of candidates' entry into the program. In phase 2, the portfolio should consist of the external self-assessment of candidates' readiness to begin the year-long internship. In phases 3 and 4, the portfolio might be the means for candidates to demonstrate their professional self-reflection.

As part of the official completion of the program, candidates present materials that give evidence of their readiness for exiting the program. Candidates create a portfolio by reviewing their work in the teacher education program and in their subject areas. This involves self-reflection and is an important step in the process. The candidates then meet with their advisers at the university to review the contents of their portfolio. The portfolio includes a videotape or videodisc of the candidate working with children or young adults, an analysis of the lesson using the five teacher education abilities, and a résumé of work experiences in K–12 settings, along with evaluations by cooperating teachers. Candidates also choose five items from their coursework, for example, something that represents their subject-area study (major), a lesson plan, a reflective writing sample, or a piece of instructional media.

SUMMARY

Case Six showed how the CT framework focuses on the abilities of the community teacher. An important subtext of the case was how it addressed the implicit question: How do you assist and assess the development of multicultural competence in practice? To adequately address this subtext, it was necessary first to articulate what multicultural competence is in terms of performance standards and then to specify what it looks like as a situated performance evaluated to a predetermined standard (i.e., as a *practice*). The standards of practice for multicultural competence were situated in the five program performance standards (and also articulated as practices in Chapter 4; see Figures 4.1 and 4.2).

The most important productive activities of the program-level system of practice are: (1) readying the practice of interns and student teachers so that they are prepared to teacher effectively on their own, (2) developing practice in schools so that the quality and richness of learning is evidenced through student achievement, and (3) promoting cultural competence. The CT framework suggests five aspects of cultural practice necessary to carry out these two productive activities (see Figures 4.1 and 4.2) that require candidates to do identity work on themselves (cf. King, 1991; Tatum, 1992) and in regard to their students (Yon, 2000).

The implication for carrying out this framework is a strong commitment to collaboration. It also requires dedication to commonly derived sets of ideas, including the old and familiar research paradigms university people are used to using. The challenge is to commit to using different methodologies and asking different questions as the demands of the work at the site dictate. These particular challenges are examined in the next chapter.

CHAPTER 8

Research *in* Practice—Creating Communities of Inquiry in Diverse Urban Communities

The interplay of subject and object, self and problem, is usually taken for granted or ignored in both qualitative and quantitative research. Yet the researcher's orientation and the definition of the situation cannot help but have ramifications for the way people are treated or thought of.
—A. Peshkin, *"The Nature of Interpretation in Qualitative Research"*

THIS CHAPTER ADDRESSES THE ROLE of research in the practices of quality teaching and learning in diverse, underserved urban schools and communities. The practice perspective developed in this book runs counter to some of the prevailing notions of teacher research and the notion of "best practices." The community teacher (CT) framework presented in these pages advocates research activity that emerges from a collaborative focus on *practice*—the site of teaching and learning—and addresses how to get results in the actual conditions in which teachers and students interact with one another. This is consistent with the relatively recent development of the research tradition known as "action research." However, the distinctions inhere not so much in the research approach as in the nature of interpretation and the questions asked (Peshkin, 2000).

THE PRACTICE OF INQUIRY IN
THE PRACTICE FRAMEWORK

In Chapter 2 I introduced the idea of *accomplished practice*, which asks the
following questions:

1. How do teachers acquire proficiencies and the *knowledge-in-practice*
   required for successfully teaching all children in a culturally responsive manner?
2. How do teachers acquire and use newly generated local knowledge to improve their teaching practice?
3. What specific changes can teachers make in how they organize
   classroom life, assess learning achievement, and support learning
   activity that will result in quality education for children in diverse
   urban communities?

Chapters 5 and 6 addressed these questions by way of illustrative cases
that demonstrated the perspective of accomplished practice in community
settings and school settings, respectively. Similarly, Chapter 7 illustrated the
practice perspective in the development of a teacher preparation program.
This chapter elaborates on accomplished practice as *research into teaching and
learning* by illustrating the roles, activities, aims, and negotiations of university, community, and school partners in what I have called a *circle of practice*.

I introduced the idea of a circle of practice in Chapter 2 and illustrated
it as five basic dimensions of pedagogical practice in Chapter 4 (see Figures
4.1 and 4.2): engagement and participation, identity development, community integrity, inquiry and reappropriation, and meaning-making. Here I
examine the practice of research inquiry in light of these dimensions.

The practice framework presented throughout this volume challenges
the notions of "one best system" and "best practices" as generic strategies
or approaches that are transportable and applicable to any teaching context. The perspective on research examined in this chapter also contests
conventional approaches to close the so-called "achievement gap" precisely
because these approaches are not framed in terms of practices, but rather
in terms of aggregate standardized test score outcomes.

NEGOTIATING TENSIONS BETWEEN RESEARCH PERSPECTIVES

A primary role for university participants in the circle of practice is to advocate *research-in-practice*, where research is embedded in the fabric of
professional activity (preferably activities that are the five community-

based pedagogies). Briefly, this idea involves a focus on practice as the tie that binds together the efforts of university researchers with parents, students, and teachers.

The notion of the circle of practice informs the research agenda for accessing both *local knowledge* and *cultural knowledge*—both of which are important for knowledge production regarding accomplished practice in diverse urban settings. Ideally, the aims of the participating university faculty members' research agendas and those of program development research converge on the five dimensions of pedagogical practice.

In this regard, this perspective on inquiry is an extension of Michele Foster's (1997) notion of *community nomination*. It is helpful to think of the emergent research paradigm as what action research would look like if it had to pass an approval board consisting of parents, community members, and community workers active in the lives of the children and youth in schools. Questions such as whether the research is valuable, purposeful, meaningful, and useful to the community ought to be addressed.

In the case of the framework, the following questions should be asked:

1. Does the research increase student engagement with learning and participation in the learning process?
2. Does the research inform how teachers can better steer young people into healthy adulthood and through the process of identity development?
3. What will be the consequence of the research activity on the ongoing process of teaching and learning?

The purpose of research inquiry ought to be to determine the accomplished practitioners in the community, and then determine the practices of inquiry and communication that extend our *cultural knowledge*. There is an element of cultural knowledge that is acquired not through research per se but through practice and reflection on practice with an appropriate set of participants. There is also an element of cultural knowledge that requires study of the heritage of African Americans, Afro Caribbeans, and every other group significantly represented in the community.

The CT research perspective described in this chapter is presented as a set of nine tensions that reveal the ongoing divergence in positionality and culture between school and university people on one hand, and parents and community agency people on the other. These tensions, listed in Figure 8.1, are basic in doing action research in community-based and school settings. This perspective acknowledges a basic overarching tension—*the knowledge production foci of university and school people diverge from those of community teachers and parents.*

Current Trends and Perspectives	Research-in-Practice Perspective
Discourse on practice is couched in terms of *"best practice"*—implying a notion of practice that is not historically, culturally, linguistically, or politically grounded.	Discourse on practice is couched in terms of *accomplished practice*—a notion of practice as it is situated in historical, cultural, and political context and grounded in authentic activity settings where achievement success can be assessed in context.
Theory and practice are regarded as *dichotomous*—as distinct and mutually exclusive ends of knowledge production.	Theory and practice are viewed as *diunital*—or inseparable in the course of inquiry and the production of new knowledge.
The unit of analysis is often either teacher practice or student outcomes but rarely the *conjoint activity* of teaching and learning. Learning is what the student produces. Instruction is what the teacher produces.	The unit of analysis is the *activity setting*— the "joint doings" of teaching practice and learner development. Knowledge production is a *joint enterprise* with *mutual engagement* of teacher and student.
The generalized research paradigm assumes *universal principles* that apply to all practices—an approach of positivistic scientific inquiry.	The challenges of effective teaching practice are taken on in locations where and with populations for whom educational practices have proven least effective—culturally and racially diverse urban communities. The uncovering of *local knowledge* is favored over the search for universal principles among the *normalized mainstream*.
It is assumed that the effectiveness of a practice can be determined irrespective of the context of activity—that it is generic and therefore transportable and replicable from one site to the next.	It is assumed that the effectiveness and quality of instructional practice should be determined only as it is *situated* in cultural, political, and historical context. Some have referred to this as *grounded theory*.
It is assumed that learning achievement is *time-specific* and occurs in all-or-none fashion—for example, as determinable by performance on a high-stakes achievement test.	It is assumed that learning achievement is *recursive,* requiring *reappropriation* of new knowledge; the development of the learner over time is assessed in a context in which *knowledge-in-use* is important.
This perspective references *practice* primarily in terms of what the teacher does, so that "teaching practices" are synonymous with "teaching strategies."	This perspective references *practice* in terms of a *joint productive activity* between and among learners, parents, and teachers, so that "practice" implies not simply a "strategy," but rather actions that are embedded in a network of people who are *mutually engaged* and are part of a *system of activity*.
This perspective permits accountability measures (e.g., aggregated scores on high-stakes assessments) to be used as indicators of successful and effective teaching and learning.	This perspective requires evaluation of the quality of teaching practice and learning achievement in the contexts and situations in which they conjointly occur.
Literacy learning and development are viewed primarily as a capacity or set of skills to be acquired.	Literacy development is linked with the processes and practices through which young people develop identity and agency.

FIGURE 8.1. Research in Practice

The practice perspective developed here is predicated on the desire to build a new common culture of interaction among school people, university people, parents, and stakeholders in the production of knowledge in partnerships. The resolution of traditional tensions is required for building a successful community of practice *and inquiry*. The resolution can only be described at this point as a series of tensions to be mediated in the ongoing development of the circle of co-participants—as working points of negotiation and as some points of contention. Those points of contention include, among other things, what should be researched, how, and by whom.

What follows is a synthesis of research perspectives described first as a set of nine tensions or polarities (see Figure 8.1). A community–university–school partnership functions well when the members can honestly acknowledge and respectfully negotiate the tensions as they move to developing an agenda of research inquiry. As I examine each divergence between community and school-based perspectives on inquiry, I propose the means by which a *circle* of practice and inquiry moves forward to become more of a *community* of practice and inquiry.

TENSION ONE–BEST PRACTICE VERSUS
ACCOMPLISHED PRACTICE

The first tension involves discourse and the contexts in which certain topics, images, and issues can be respectfully raised. One aspect of this tension is a difference in views regarding what constitutes good practice. From the community perspective, good practice is always situated and grounded in the present with the children in front of you.

The university and school perspective tends to see "best practice" as universal—something one reads about in the research literature or something one recalls that "research says." In discussions of the action team, this tension surfaces when the parents point out that the best practice suggested by the university person or the teacher is not necessarily the best practice for the children in the school or program. This *practice perspective on research* is contrary to how many culturally mainstream teachers view practice. They have been conditioned to find "best practices" in their trade journals, professional development workshops, and professional meetings.

One example of the results of this tension was the children's literature controversy in Case One. The "best practice" in this case was to have children role-play as a way of engaging them in the topic of freedom struggle. But this "best practice" in the context of the case actually ends up degrading any authentic meaning of freedom struggle. The treatment of the book, the selection of activities, and, most important, the exclusion of voices that should have been heard in the development of curriculum led to a trivialization of the topic, and a demeaning representation of freedom struggle—demonstrating the glitches in the way many culturally mainstream teachers, who have been conditioned to find "best practices" in their trade journals, professional development workshops, and professional meetings, view practice.

A second example comes from Case Four. Ms. Mercer adopted what she considered "best practice" by providing a powerful experience to stimulate participation by the introduction of the Billie Holiday song "Strange Fruit." She was following what is regarded to be best practice from the standpoint of literacy teaching. She was applying what she had learned from her extensive work in teaching reading—it was instructional principle #4 from Hoffman and colleagues (2000): "Effective reading instruction encourages students to engage aesthetically with text" (p. 28). However, this "best practice" principle was superseded by a community practice principle that required taking into account how the African American students might experience the introduction of the topic of lynching. What transactions move a circle of practice to a community of practice when Ms. Mercer moves to become a more accomplished practitioner?

In the conference, Mr. DuBose explained how abruptly introducing the subject of racial oppression into a lesson might make an African American high school student feel. He pointed out that this is a common experience of Black children, who too often are assaulted by curricula in which African Americans are invisible in U.S. history until the topic of slavery is introduced. Mr. DuBose shared with Ms. Mercer the sense of shame and anger it produced for history to be so distorted as to tacitly suggest that Black history began with slavery. He hastened to add in their conversation that her lesson was not necessarily an instance of the inappropriate introduction of a racial text, but he wanted to query her about the consideration she had given to the impact the topic might have on the students.

For instance, had she considered how the introduction of such a topic might have immediately positioned one group of students with respect to the other? One group of students might immediately be identified as victims and another group identified as perpetrators. Had she anticipated the range of emotional reactions? Guilt, indifference, and denial are possible reactions from the White students; shame, anger, and denial are possible reactions from African American students.

The point to be made here is not simply about reflective practice or multicultural competence. It is not merely a matter of being a multiculturally reflective practitioner who regularly anticipates different perspectives. The point is that accomplished practice by a community teacher involves a deeper cultural inquiry as to the basis of that anticipation. Good practice here is *not just about anticipating,* but also the means of checking to be sure that your judgments are accurate. Instead of guessing what the anticipated responses might be, it should be a professional act to find out by whatever means are appropriate—conversations with parents, colleagues of color, or the students themselves. This underscores the importance of a community of practice that really supports the accomplished practice of a community teacher.

In a circle of practice, this new awareness for Ms. Mercer might be a one-shot deal. In the conversation with Mr. DuBose, it might merely have been an instance of his making her aware that some children might take offense at the topic. Ms. Mercer might duly note this, but as a consequence she might be less likely to risk using a racial text in the future even when she knows she is sacrificing opportunities to connect with her students. In a community of practice, however, Ms. Mercer is more likely to have this disposition of monitoring become a regular part of her practice. In a community of practice, she can continue her more daring, innovative, and on-the-edge attempts to connect with her students without worrying about the reprisals and misunderstandings that are always a risk in dealing with racialized text. Why? It is because she would have sources of cultural knowledge to inform her practice and to draw on when making important pedagogical decisions.

TENSION TWO—DICHOTOMOUS VERSUS DIUNITAL THEORY

The second tension concerns the differences in discourse on practice. In the practice framework developed here, I argue for accomplished *practice*— a notion of practice as it is situated in historical, cultural, and political context. It is a notion of practice that is grounded in authentic activity settings in which achievement success can be assessed in context. Theory and practice are viewed as *diunital*—or inseparable in the course of inquiry and the production of new knowledge.

Here is an example of this second conflicting tension. A young faculty member at the university, Mr. Barber, who was hired for his expertise and research in elementary reading, began working with a number of teachers at the Martin Luther King Pilot School on improving reading fluency. He was helping the third- and fourth-grade teachers revise their literacy learning routines toward a model that stressed the development of fluency, which he was currently researching. He worked with the teachers to revise the traditional basal reading lessons based on the districts' limited selection of material and consisting mostly of a more traditional directed-reading activity. The new system that Mr. Barber proposed combined elements of free-choice reading and shared reading between student "reading pals" to boost fluency.

All the teachers were happy with the new reading system. Then Mr. Barber proposed that they test the efficacy of their new system. He secured preliminary permission to collect data as part of his research agenda. However, when he indicated that he wanted to continue the more traditional reading system in one of the classes, so as to have a proper control group to match against the students using the new approach, the teachers became very upset. Mr. Barber argued that he needed a control group and experimental group for his research evaluating the new reading program. The teachers in the school, although eager to work with the new program, were opposed to evaluating it in the way that Mr. Barber proposed. They were opposed to looking at the literacy practice and evaluating its success in comparison to the traditional basal program.

The teacher of the designated "control" class, Ms. McMurphy, in particular was outspoken in arguing with Mr. Barber. She said, "I understand the nature of research. But look at it from my perspective. If I think this new system is better than the traditional one, what right do I have to give my children anything but the best? Mr. Douglas, a parent from the Martin Luther King School with a high school equivalency diploma, offered an insightful and succinct statement that went right to the heart of the conflict—the nature of positivistic empirical educational research and the issue of generalizability. Speaking to Mr. Barber in the meeting, he said, "Here's the trouble with the way you do research. For you, if it works over there but not over here, it's still good enough for you. When you write up results, you give reasons why maybe it doesn't work over here, but then you want to go ahead and use it over here as if it had worked. I'm saying, if it doesn't work right here where I'm at, it's not worth much and it's time to go back to the drawing board!"

For community people, theory and practice tend to be viewed as *diunital*—or inseparable in the course of inquiry and the production of new knowledge. In other words, for this group there is not much value or point to talking about theory that does not relate to some real endeavor, problem, or enterprise. University and school partners are far more apt to talk about theory as though it had value independent of activity. This difference shows up in many disagreements between the two groups, with parents being exasperated with any fealty to a system of ideas that has already proven ineffective, irrelevant, or even destructive to their children.

In both tensions discussed thus far, the movement toward resolution of basic differences is through discussion. Discursive practice—the deliberate and systematic articulation of foundational differences among participants contemplating a research project—should be nurtured as part of the community building the group does.

TENSION THREE—ANALYSIS OF PHENOMENA VERSUS HUMAN SYSTEMS

The third tension concerns how parents and community people view the activity of doing research, its purposes and uses. In the research proposals of university partners, the *unit of analysis* is often either teacher activity or student performance, but rarely the *conjoint activity* of teaching and learning as combined teacher and learner performances. From a traditional research perspective, learning and teaching can be seen as independent products or processes—learning achievement is what the student produces and instruction is what the teacher produces. By contrast, from a parent's perspective, the unit of analysis does not split apart process from product. In this view the unit of analysis is the *activity setting*—the "joint doings" of teaching practice and learner development. Knowledge production is a *joint enterprise* with *mutual engagement* of teacher and student.

Movement toward resolving the tension occurs through careful articulation of meaningful inquiry—research that serves the interests of improving the practices of teaching and learning.

TENSION FOUR—UNIVERSAL PRINCIPLES VERSUS LOCAL KNOWLEDGE

The fourth tension is related to the second regarding the uses, development, and purposes of theory. The unit of analysis or the locus of inquiry for community people, parents, and families tends to be the *activity setting*—the "joint doings" of teaching practice and learner development. Knowledge production from this perspective ought to be a joint enterprise with *mutual engagement* of teacher and student. This disposition developed, in part, from an unfortunate history of the way in which university researchers or school people conducted their "action research"—leaving little legacy of assistance and taking the knowledge produced to some research journal instead of back into the community where it was unearthed. This is a legacy that university and school people still strive to overcome.

TENSION FIVE—CONTEXT FREE VERSUS SITUATED THEORY

The fifth tension, like the first four, involves the intersection of theory and context. The traditional view of theory is that it is universal and generalizable to many different situations and contexts. The assumption is that the value of theory in teaching practice can be determined irrespective of the context of activity—that theory is generic and therefore transportable and replicable from one site to the next. By contrast, the assumption from the community teacher perspective is that the effectiveness and quality of instructional practice should be determined only as it is *situated* in a cultural, political, and historical context. Some have referred to this as grounded theory or situated cognition (Brown, Collins, & Duguid, 1989). The community-oriented perspective on theory in practice is that the focus of partnership should be on developing effective teaching practice in locations where and with populations for whom educational practices have proven least effective—in urban communities with culturally and racially diverse populations. The uncovering of *local knowledge* is favored over the search for universal principles among the *normalized mainstream*.

TENSION SIX—SEQUENCED VERSUS RECURSIVE LEARNING PROCESS

A sixth tension concerns perspectives on learning. Parents tend to assume that learning achievement is *recursive*, requiring *reappropriation* of new knowledge and repetition of teaching. They do not expect a one-time teaching event to "take hold"; they expect that repeated reminders and occasions for practice will be necessary. Yet this is exactly the perspective on learning enacted in many classrooms, where learning is viewed as a sequential, all-or-none set of experiences.

TENSION SEVEN—STRATEGIES VERSUS SYSTEMS OF PRACTICE

A seventh contrast in perspectives concerns the idea of practice. It is related to the prior tension concerning perspectives on learning. From the framework advocated in these pages and from the perspective of many parents and community partners, teaching practice is (or ought to be) a *joint productive activity* between and among teachers, parents, and learners, so that "practice" implies not simply a "strategy," but rather actions that are embedded in a network of people who are *mutually engaged* and are part of a *system of activity*. This is expressed by parents' desire to be "on the same page" as the teacher regarding the performance expectations of their children.

By contrast, university and school partners frequently view *practice* primarily in terms of only what the teacher does, so that "teaching practices" are synonymous with "teaching strategies."

TENSION EIGHT—AGGREGATE VERSUS
ACTUAL ACHIEVEMENT

Perhaps the most critical tension in developing a community of practice concerns the evaluation of achievement performance. From the community-oriented perspective, evaluation of the quality of teaching practice and learning achievement must be made in the contexts and situations in which they conjointly occur. School and university people tend to operate from a perspective of high-stakes accountability, which means accepting aggregated scores on high-stakes assessments as legitimate accountability measures to be used as indicators of successful and effective teaching and learning. Parents and community agency directors, on the other hand, resist the tendency to frame solutions in terms of policy measures instead of actual achievement. Specifically, why should efforts to improve student achievement take the form of intensive test remediation instead of a focus on the curriculum proper? The decision to institute a remediation program is a policy decision, not a curricular one.

TENSION NINE—LITERACY FOR SKILLS VERSUS
LITERACY FOR LIFE

The disposition toward high-stakes testing shows up in the final tension. Literacy development is linked with the processes and practices through which young people develop identity and agency. Too often in the public schools, literacy learning and development are viewed primarily as a capacity or set of skills to be acquired. As a result, in the effort to close the achievement gap, there is an overemphasis on decontextualized reading skills in the form of word attack and letter-to-sound correspondence (phonics) at the expense of literacy as meaning-making.

From the CT perspective, literacy learning and development are more substantially linked with the processes and practices through which young people develop identity and agency. This conflict can be illustrated by the aftermath of the controversy described in Case One. Later, Ms. Britt argued with Ms. Hall about her selection of the book and how it could have contributed to the children's trivial and inaccurate interpretations of slavery and the narrative of Frederick Douglass. Ms. Hall at first defended the book, *Frederick Douglass: The Last Day of Slavery* (Miller, 1995), particularly since it had won an award. Ms. Britt said, "Just because a book wins an award doesn't automatically make it good literature or appropriate for curriculum. Would the author really have us believe that field hands sat down in the middle of the day for a lunch break? Would he really have us believe that Frederick Douglass, as a field hand, read a book in the grass on his lunch break?" When Ms. Britt pointed out a few other historical inaccuracies—based on Douglass's own account in his first autobiography—and some of the insipid imagery of slave life, Ms. Hall began to appreciate the perspective of an African American educator.

In a calmer conversation later between the two, Ms. Britt was able to show Ms. Hall what was problematic about the book from an African American perspective. Ms. Hall began to see how the young Douglass was positioned as "different" and "exceptional" from other enslaved Africans because he apparently was, according to the fictionalized account in the book, the only one who walked with his head up, *the only one* to dream about freedom, and *the only one* who dared to resist authority.

SUMMARY

This chapter examined some of the conflicts and barriers to forming a CT community of practice in regard to doing research. The conflicts were described as a set of nine tensions between university and school perspectives on the one hand, and community and critical perspectives on the other hand. The CT framework advocates that these tensions be made explicit as community–school–university partners come together to organize the research agenda of the partnership.

CHAPTER 9

Assessing Teacher Performance— Performance-Based Teacher Assessment

The development of practice takes time, but what defines a community of practice in its temporal dimension is not just a matter of a specific minimum amount of time. Rather, it is a matter of sustaining enough mutual engagement in pursuing an enterprise together to share some significant learning. From this perspective, communities of practice can be thought of as shared histories of learning.

—*E. Wenger*, Communities of Practice

THIS CHAPTER EXAMINES PERFORMANCE ASSESSMENT of teachers and systems of teaching, especially as it applies to creating an urban-focused and community-dedicated school of education. The issue is how to create a performance-based system of teacher assessment from, and for, practice in diverse settings. There are a number of performance-based approaches to evaluating teacher quality, including the performance assessment approaches of the National Board for Professional Teaching Standards (NBPTS) and the Interstate New Teacher Assessment and Support Consortium (INTASC). Additionally, the National Council for Accreditation of Teacher Education (NCATE) has set new professional standards for examining the frameworks for performance assessment in teacher preparation (NCATE, 2000). Both program standards and teaching practice standards need to be examined in light of urban teaching and professional development schools (PDSs). How does a program develop an assessment system in light of this external set of standards? In this chapter I develop five critical points of inquiry to use in designing an assessment system.

I begin first by noting that, in the teaching standards, there is a general script of accomplished practice that is largely structured by the process of performance assessment based on portfolios and artifacts of practice. This in itself is not a bad thing, but it can be limiting and overprescriptive as a model for designing an assessment system for an individual school of education. What have not been fully addressed are the inconsistencies between the standards-based model of accomplished practice and actual accomplished urban practice in diverse settings. The community teacher (CT) framework is predicated on how to address the missing pieces in the general script when we turn to urban classrooms.

THE STANDARDS-BASED GENERAL SCRIPT OF PRACTICE

The general script of accomplished practice for the community teacher needs to be much more specific about the requirements of cultural competency, the ethics of caring, and cultural-political agency than those provided by national organizations. Accomplished practice for successful teaching in urban contexts looks different from that of the usual model of teacher preparation, which often seems most appropriate for candidates in a monocultural, culturally mainstream suburban context.

Accomplished practice for the next generation of teachers requires both a healing function and a health-maintenance function, to use a medical analogy. Accomplished practice for the urban teacher has to be the "holistic medicine" of teaching and learning, which refuses to "treat" only the symptoms of the disease. In medicine there is a difference between the practice of an intern and that of a resident. The differences are in the accomplishments of practice—one is a more accomplished practitioner than the other. Experience aids accomplished practice, but it is not the same thing. A teacher who has been in the system for 20 or 30 years is not necessarily an accomplished teacher. Longevity is not accomplishment, unless one has such a cynical view of urban teaching that one sees mere longevity of service as indicative of meritorious service.

Just as there ought to be verifiable differences among interns, residents, and full-fledged doctors, so should there be among beginning, competent, and accomplished practitioners in teaching. Unlike doctors, teachers are held accountable for more than they are responsible for. Doctors are held accountable principally for the symptoms or disorders they treat, not for the general health of the patient. The number of healthy people in their charge is not used to measure their success as medical practitioners. Teachers, on the other hand, seem to be held accountable for both—the "sick patients," as indicated by the number of students at or below some cutoff score on a standardized achievement test, as well as the "healthy patients," since all students are expected to make achievement progress.

The initiatives such as those of the NBPTS and INTASC provide a framework for getting a handle on the differences in accomplished practice—a term which actually comes from the NBPTS. These organizations work with the idea of a continuum of practice from beginning to competent to accomplished practice. The indicators for improving practice mentioned in the preceding chapters are also codified in the program standards of NCATE and in the performance standards of INTASC and the NBPTS. Therefore, a good beginning step for creating an assessment system for an urban-focused and community-committed teacher education program would be to articulate the differences in practice between an accomplished practitioner and a competent practitioner using these frameworks. There are limits, however, to how useful these standards and indicators are in building a truly effective urban pedagogy and school of education.

Standards provide the means for making judgments about whether teaching performance or program performance constitutes accomplished practice. They are not articulations of accomplished practice themselves, but tools for appraising practice. I have argued that the articulation of teaching and program standards must involve the participation of a wider circle of people than is typically the case in traditional teacher preparation.

Just as years of experience in the field are not the same thing as accomplished practice, neither are the five NBPTS standards or the ten INTASC standards articulations of accomplished practice. If they were, there would be no further need for reform of teacher preparation, for all that would be necessary would be to have candidates and teachers "meet" those standards. Obviously, however, standards are not practices. Standards do not specify teacher/learner activity, but the quality of that activity. Like most things worthwhile, the devil is in the details. It is up to professional units to specify the *details of doing* that constitute a program and to develop an assessment system that reveals how good "the doing" is relative to the standards.

PRINCIPLES OF PERFORMANCE ASSESSMENT

The following five principles characterize a strategy for developing a performance assessment system for producing community teachers. They provide a design for making explicit the challenges of evaluating and scaffolding the development of the desired practices for candidates in light of state, national, and local imperatives. The principles are ordered in a developmental progression for the task of implementing teaching performance assessments. Associated with each principle are a number of key questions that, in my experience, must be successfully engaged.

PRINCIPLE ONE

The teacher education unit must determine collectively what it values as professional ability, skill, and knowledge. In the case of an urban-focused, community-dedicated school of education, the faculty members and stakeholders will want to consider those abilities, skills, and knowledge that make a good urban teacher. The circle of practice, including parents and community members, faces several specific questions en route to creating a performance assessment system for community teachers: (1) How will we settle on what we value as pedagogical ability? (2) Who should be included in these conversations? (3) By what means will standards be set?

As argued earlier, determining the qualities of accomplished practice for the unit is more than simply a matter of determining what is to be expected of candidates on completion of program. Although it is true that some of this work is guided by INTASC principles, by the NBPTS standards, and by state standards, the essence of what constitutes accomplished practice for the communities served is not likely to be prescribed by these standards. A unit must also articulate performance standards that might profitably begin with modeling the practice of community teachers nominated by constituencies in the community beyond universities and schools.

The work done in a circle of practice is the articulation of a common ground and common meaning. This involves tackling questions such as: (1) How will the circle of practice articulate what it values in terms of what teachers do? (2) How *does* a unit come to common agreement on what "a good teacher" is? Note that the first of these questions signals a performance perspective of the CT framework—moving away from articulating pedagogical readiness solely according to the sequence of courses one has completed in curriculum, methods, human development, and the like. It is equally important, however, not to fall into the trap of considering only observable behaviors—which is the reason for emphasizing *practice* as the unit of analysis. Designating discrete behaviors not only leads down a path of infinite lists but also makes it difficult to specify the complex, rich pedagogical dispositions that are part of accomplished practice.

A colleague of mine, Susan Melnick, has often reminded those in teacher preparation that the critical forgotten quality in the mantra "what teachers know and are able to do" is what they are *disposed* to do. The second of these questions urges deliberate collaboration on the task of generating performance standards. For example, at the middle school where Ms. Mercer teaches, parents have become increasingly insistent that the teachers take action on the fact that the new cohort of sixth-graders, as a group, seems not to like reading or writing. Through the parent council and individually, parents have been applying pressure on teachers to do something. Although they are frustrated that the school does not seem to be acting with the appropriate urgency and seriousness, the situation is an opportunity to codify important qualities of practice. The university participants in these discussions want candidates to learn how to forge working relationships with parents out of this urgency and to see parents as collaborators in the development of the school rather than as people asked to simply reinforce school policy and expectations. The ability to work collaboratively with parents on a schoolwide concern may thus be incorporated as a performance standard for the university's teacher education program.

PRINCIPLE TWO

What the unit values as professional ability, skill, and knowledge, it must articulate as performance. Once the circle of practice has some common agreement about the qualities of accomplished practice that their community teachers must possess, it is necessary to state those qualities in terms of performance so that it is possible to assess the degree to which candidates and teachers display those qualities of practice. There are three key questions collaborators in a circle of practice should ask at this phase of developing the assessment plan. First, how do you state good practice as performance? One productive way to accomplish this is with videotaped archives of accomplished practice or instances of good teaching. It is often useful to work backwards from a teaching performance that has produced excellent results to identify what elements of it constitute good practice.

Second, how do you state "intangible qualities" of good teaching as performance? Important "intangible" qualities may not be observable in a single viewing of a videotape or even in a series of classroom visits. The quality may be that the teacher "teaches every single child in his or her classroom to read"—which is something one cannot actually observe as a set of behaviors, but is determined by other kinds of evidence. Herein lies the challenge of articulating desirable practice as performance—determining what counts as evidence for good teaching performance. Parents and community members often prove to be more capable of specifying the intangibles of a community teacher's practice than professional educators, because they usually relate to qualities of the relationship between teachers and students that escape the "professional" lens of educators. The deliberations in the circle of practice need to be continually mindful of this fact.

Finally, how will the group clearly communicate the performances you articulate to candidates, colleagues, and the wider community? Close association and collaboration with parent circles and the school parent council is important—and might even be articulated as a performance standard for both candidates and the program in general.

PRINCIPLE THREE

Whatever professional and pedagogical abilities your unit values, it must assist candidates in acquiring those professional abilities. In other words, once the unit specifies the professional abilities, it must then determine the means for assisting candidates and teachers in their acquisition of those abilities. This task can be organized by three questions. First, what experiences move candidates toward mastery of the abilities? Second, what are the criteria that separate beginning level from advanced level of ability on the performances the unit values? Criteria are necessary not only for defining and describing the desired performance but also for distinguishing between good practice and better practice, and between better practice and best practice. Third, what combination of field experiences and coursework is optimal for moving students toward advanced levels of performance? An example of how this might be set up was provided in Chapter 7.

Sandra Hurley's enrollment in the first course of the teacher education sequence placed her in a combined field work and coursework context, creating the opportunity for her to demonstrate the capacities she already has in relation to the five performance standards for becoming a community teacher. Her teaching practice was assisted with a "starter kit"— a teaching script that scaffolded her successful interaction with children. Working side by side with accomplished community teachers provided Sandra the opportunity to see a script of accomplished practice and to use it as a model for her own.

PRINCIPLE FOUR

Whatever performances your unit assists, it must publicly and explicitly assess. This task can be organized by three questions. First, what counts as *evidence* in the performance of candidates as they progress from beginning levels of the ability to advanced levels? Second, do candidates, colleagues, and collaborators know, and work with, your standards of performance in both clinical and classroom settings? Finally, are the unit's performance standards at the center of teacher preparation learning activity? That is, do they define what your unit does with and for teacher candidates to help them become teachers? Assessment as learning is important here—candidates are capable of achieving what is clearly articulated, modeled, and scaffolded in their own performance.

The key for realizing this principle is that the written documents communicate the performance standards by a living document—something used in teaching, assisting, assessing performance, and self-assessment.

PRINCIPLE FIVE

Whatever performances your unit values, it must make explicit the means by which candidates are assisted in achieving them. This task is organized by three questions. First, what counts as evidence that performances are progressing from beginning-level ability to advanced-level ability in a candidate? Second, in what ways are the professional and pedagogical abilities reflected in other venues of your unit? Are they manifested in the university courses students are taking? Are they central to the conversations with partners in setting up PDS relationships and clinical sites? Do they connect with candidates' liberal arts coursework? Finally, what counts as evidence that the performances you expect of candidates are worthwhile, valuable, significant, and important?

APPRAISAL OF PRACTICE IN THE COMMUNITY TEACHER FRAMEWORK

The practice orientation expressed in this volume specifies a particular quality of reflection that I have designated *appraisal of practice,* an extension of the well-known notion of the reflective practitioner (Dewey, 1933; Schön, 1989). Appraisal of practice is the key principle in the entire conceptual framework for the community teacher and community partnership approach to teacher preparation described thus far. The process of developing an assessment system outlined by the five principles above should result in a means for appraising both individual performance and program outcomes to prepare the community teacher.

In the Introduction, where I characterized the crisis of knowledge in teacher education, the fundamental disconnection between policy and practice noted was the absence of *appraisal of practice.* The crux of the crisis of knowledge is the absence of careful, critical, and appropriate assessment of the systems of practice proposed as reform measures. Policy makers are unable to successfully follow the practical outcomes of their policy decisions because they are not in a position to assess practice in the cultural and historical contexts in which it occurs. Appraisal of practice is the ignition key to effective, transformative teaching. Every good reflective practitioner assesses his or her activity in light of the outcomes for learners or clients. However, *appraisal of practice* requires that this self-assessment be systematic and contain certain features.

In Chapter 2 I argued for a *system of practice* in which *assessment of professional work* is the key to collaboration among community, university, and school personnel on teaching practice. *Professional practice* must be assessed as both *instructional activity* and *professional activity* in conjunction with the achievement outcomes of the students served. Otherwise, nothing can be said about the worth or value of the practice, because it is not possible to determine whether the failures lie with the practices themselves or with the poor implementation. Programs that do not situationally or culturally fit the community of learners and teachers will not meet their needs, regardless of how well the programs work elsewhere or whether they are on the approved list of education reforms.

I have defined *practice* as a generic system of activity that includes not only what professionals do in a given setting but also what they are disposed to do in similar settings. A given *teaching practice* is recognizable as a pattern or a system of activity in which the aims of the teacher are explicit, the context of the mutual participation of teacher and learning is specified, and the achievement outcomes are clear and verifiable in relation to the aims.

Assessment is fundamental to the development of any activity that we deem worthwhile. Whether regarding an individual, a team, or an organizational system, effective assessment always proceeds from an account of performance. Next, there is always a judgment of the performance according to criteria. Not every activity is a performance. Figure skaters or gymnasts warming up their routines are not engaged in performances. The activity involved in warming up is not the performance. It is, however, when the routines are done in front of judges who assess their performance according to mutually understood criteria.

Analogously for teaching, the difference between an activity and an effective performance is whether the instructional activity is appraised and receives feedback. Whether feedback comes from a colleague, a mentor teacher, or self-assessment, teaching is a performance when it is assessed according to criteria-related achievement outcomes for the children. When the assessment of the performance includes criteria relating to the appropriateness of the activity to situational and cultural contexts and success over time, then the activity is called a *practice*. A practice is a performance evaluated in context.

There are not very many assessment systems in teacher education that link the evaluation of a teacher's performance explicitly to students' achievement performances. Nonetheless, this link is urged by the new national agenda. Throughout this text the importance of assessing practice as it is linked to student outcomes has been emphasized. In Chapter 2, the movement from a focus on specific individuals' practices (designated "low focus on practice" in Figure 2.4) to a focus on generic accomplished practice is what partly determines the level or progression of the partnership arrangements depicted in Figure 2.4.

At the micro level of accountability, the assessment of an individual's practice ought to be made through performance—both that of the teacher and that of the students. The meso level of accountability refers to the practice of a group of individuals—a team or other grouping of teachers who share professional and instructional practices. Here the assessment of collective practice is made through the evaluation of programs (curriculum, reading programs, etc.) and projects. However, the determination of their quality is still based on the outcomes of students, registered by an assessment of classroom practice. In other words, one determines the quality of programs and projects based on the quality of instructional practice of the individuals participating.

At the macro level, the evaluation of institutions is also based on the assessment at the previous levels: Evaluation of an institution is based on an assessment of the quality of its programs and projects. Thus, appraisal of practice from individual teacher, to collective of teachers, to programs and projects, to institutions is based on performance.

SUMMARY

This chapter examined performance assessment and discussed its significance in light of promoting quality teaching, both in terms of the new national agenda and in terms of the community teacher model. The key idea is the relationship between practice and performance—if we want to evaluate practice, then we have to assess performance. The challenge that was discussed concerned articulating the appropriate criteria for assessing performance. Five principles were proposed for how a professional unit constructs aspects of practice that are community-sensitive, culturally responsive, and urban-focused. The main principle was the inclusion of a wide community of participants that can better inform accomplished urban practice than the smaller circle of higher education faculty. Finally, appraisal of practice was described. Appraisal of practice assesses how well a school, a partnership, or a classroom functions as a *system* that is designed to bring about desirable outcomes for children. Community teachers successfully appraise practice—their own and their colleagues'.

CHAPTER 10

Building Institutional Coalitions for Renewal

The alignment strategy that Federal, state, and local policy-makers have pursued to make K–12 education more coherent has typically tried to pull together features of different external systems—standards, assessment, curriculum, teacher preparation and the like. The truth is, however, that different parts of the same system—elementary schools, middle schools, and secondary schools—rarely communicate with each other about educational goals and purposes.
  —Preliminary Report of the National Commission
  on the High School Senior Year

WITH THE COMMUNITY TEACHER FRAMEWORK put forth in this book, I have attempted to describe how we should go about building institutional coalitions for the renewal of teaching, learning, and youth development in urban schools and communities. I have formulated the community teacher (CT) conceptual framework for building new systems of practice, given the current constraints and opportunities in the current educational landscape.

Within the CT framework, I have elaborated on the idea of creating effective collaboration and accomplished teaching in urban schools. I did this from a perspective that differs from those of contemporary frameworks of school reform, such as John Goodlad's (1994) centers of pedagogy and the professional development school (PDS) notion of the Holmes Group (1986, 1990). The difference is subtle but important. Rather than approaching the work from the standpoint of policy change and interinstitutional work, I have approached it from the standpoint of community development—of children, their teachers, their families, their shared systems of practice, and their common activity to fashion a better democratic public life. In truth, the most productive and important elements of recent approaches to school reform boil down some version of this key idea of systematic community building. The most successful instances of educational renewal have long since moved beyond the binary collaboration of university and school partners to include movements and community organization (Shirley, 1997). Collaborative partnership among community, school, and higher education for the renewal of all three venues is the central idea now.

PDS types of partnerships flounder with respect to community-based education because of the difficulty of creating true communities of practice. Partnership enterprises, which include only professional educators from school and university sites, can have only limited success in urban schools and communities as long as they continue to limit the terms of collaboration. The PDS agenda does not include a wider sharing of responsibility for, and commitment to, the development and achievement of African American and Hispanic children, who are the majority in large urban school systems.

BACK TO THE FUTURE: CENTERS OF PEDAGOGY

The PDS idea itself, as articulated by the Holmes Group, is no more an innovation than the institution of high school was at the turn of the twentieth century. The idea of "centers of pedagogy" can be traced back to John Dewey, who in 1896 proposed a department of pedagogy at the University of Chicago. John Goodlad and others have revived the idea in the last couple of decades. But the concept still excludes important constituencies. Even the most recent writings on the idea of centers of pedagogy (Patterson, Michelli, & Pacheco, 1999) refer to only faculty in schools and colleges of education and faculty in the arts and sciences. There is no mention of parents, youth workers, or educators not bound to universities or public schools. The centers of pedagogy agenda is a movement in the right direction, but is limited by its exclusion of wider community movements for educational renewal.

The movement for university–school collaboration has not moved appreciably from the charge of PDSs emerging from the Holmes Group to "invent an institutional coalition that will bring *all the required forces* together—universities, schools of education and public schools" (Holmes Group, 1990, pp. 2–3; emphasis added). What I have always objected to in the PDS agenda is the assumption that universities, schools of education, and public schools constitute "all the required forces." The Holmes Group statement excludes community movements, social justice movements, parent movements, and groups active in the struggle for quality education. At its worst, the statement communicates arrogance and professional elitism that has, as I stated earlier, prompted the epithet of the "great White school reform" from my colleague. At best, the statement represents a (hopefully unintentional) narrow perspective that hinders the recognition of real struggle for educational renewal. A view so narrow that it fails to recognize the social and cultural contexts of the struggles for quality education that are, in some cases, centuries old (as is the case for African Americans) will always fall short. The exclusiveness of mutual renewal of only university and school personnel is a critique I have made elsewhere (Murrell, 1998) and will not be repeated here other than to note that the persistence of this dichotomy has its own historical roots (cf. Patterson et al., 1999).

The unfortunate legacy is that the PDS aim of "mutual renewal" is unlikely to be realized as long as university and school faculty do not truly share their practice. Where is the "mutuality" when only the school faculty is held accountable for the performance of their children and their schools? Shared practices that produce mutually valued learning outcomes among teachers become *instructional systems*. In the CT framework, these activities are called *instructional activity settings*. But there are also instructional systems that link school settings with home and community settings. This is the sense in which we have to push for "mutual renewal" and development. The specifics of how well systems like these work in a particular context are determined by the professional educators responsible for student achievement and development in those contexts. Adapting these systems to promote learning achievement is the work of circles of practice in the school—which should include, in addition to teachers, parents, arts and sciences faculty from the university partners, and community educators from the community partners.

MICRO-LEVEL DEVELOPMENT

At the micro level of instructional systems in the CT model, curriculum and instructional delivery constitute the focus of circles of practice. In the more traditional approaches to teacher education, the performance expectations for both candidates and practicing teachers are set by many external constraints, such as state competencies and professional development requirements for advanced certification. The problem that this creates is the tendency for more traditional programs to adopt the state's competencies and requirements as *the* performance standards expected of program completers. As we have seen in the development of the CT framework in Chapters 3 and 4, this is not good enough for effective practice in diverse urban settings. In the CT framework, by contrast, performance standards are based on the requirements of exemplary practice in culturally diverse urban schools and communities. As was illustrated in Chapter 7, the performance standards for effective practice are established independently of state competencies and in accordance with what effective practice requires in the urban contexts where teachers teach and learn to teach. The state competencies are not ignored, but rather are appropriately incorporated in the overall assessment plan of the professional unit.

Statewide competencies rarely articulate performances that are specific enough to provide the program performance standards for the professional unit (although the University of Western Oregon, the University of Kentucky, and the University of Texas, for example, are experiencing success doing so). In the more traditional teacher education program, diversity is too often addressed by creating a number of experiences or courses designed to improve the "multicultural competence" of candidates. A frequent problem with this approach is that the specific performances and practices of multicultural competence are not articulated. In contrast, the CT framework requires that the articulation of the performances precede the formulation and assessment of performance standards related to effective work in diverse settings.

Accomplished practice in culturally and racially diverse contexts is far from being "all worked out," even though the basic frameworks of culturally responsive teaching, ethnically centered pedagogy, and multicultural education offer starting points for circles of practice to focus on diversity issues. In the CT framework, a principal function of a circle of practice is *inquiry*. Action research, curricular explorations, and experimentatal instructional systems are important professional activities.

The *professional activity settings*, where research and inquiry into teaching should take place, become an important system of activity for circles of practice to organize. Although virtually every articulation of educational reform validates the idea of values and the idea of "communities of practice and inquiry," much needs to be done to develop systems that span the micro and meso levels of school activity.

THE MESO LEVEL AND THE IMPORTANCE
OF SHARED PRACTICE

What makes the articulation of practice important is that it makes explicit the multiple levels of entry points into practice. There are multiple locations of expertise in the instructional practices expected of the competent teacher. Wenger (1999) calls this "legitimate peripheral participation." It is the position a novice can assume, alongside an experienced practitioner, in the enactment of practice; it is where the novice can both learn and contribute. It is precisely the Vygotskian idea of the zone of proximal development.

Case Three provided an example of the practice base on elevating literacy learning. There is a level at which freshmen can participate in this instructional practice that permits their learning about pedagogy, about literacy, and about the social and cultural contexts of teaching that are possible at the same time that they can make a meaningful contribution to the learning of children. This practice orientation contrasts with the old apprenticeship model, which locates all teacher training at the micro level instead of recognizing the need for interinstitutional and interprofessional interaction (the meso level). Rather than expecting one person to act as a mentor teacher, in guiding the novice teacher, the responsibility of mentorship is owned and acted upon by several more capable members of the instructional group. Mentor teachers or cooperating teachers have not cornered the market on good teaching, but they do provide the context in which novice teachers can get assistance on their practice.

THE MACRO LEVEL OF PRACTICE AND
THE CULTURE OF THE SCHOOL

The CT model stresses a new perspective on practice. Why must assessment and evaluation be predicated on practice? It is because the essential elements of successful practice would be ignored without the context of interpersonal relationships and interactions. The literature on organizational theory is predicated on the idea that a design of human systems that does not take account of the culture of the organization is not likely to achieve the desired results. Sarason (1971) is one well-known educator associated with this idea, as are Hargreaves and Fullan (1996) and Senge (1995). The jumping-off point for this book has been the limitation of this work with regard to *practice in diverse urban settings,* which extends beyond but definitely includes the focus on the culture of the school. This is a limitation because the culture of the school—the bureaucratic culture—is only a part of the cultural scene. This was articulated as the connection between meso levels and macro levels of activity and development.

The new national agenda has elicited an increased interest in partnerships, collaboratives, and educational reform networks as the institutional structures compatible with national and local initiatives for school reform. As a result, considerable attention has been given to the types of organizations of government, community-based agencies, school districts, and institutions of higher education that are required to enact locally and nationally legislated school reform.

If there is to be a greater integration of federal- and state-mandated performance standards, the systems of practice responsible for this integration need to be of appropriate scale and level to incorporate representation of schools, universities, community agencies, and state departments of education. In the trajectory model in Figure 2.4, this is represented by the top circle, labeled Coalition of Community Partnerships and PDSs on Teaching Quality. This macro-level system of practice exists in a number of forms. Among these forms are networks, coalitions, and collaboratives. The Massachusetts Coalition for Teacher Quality and Student Achievement and the El Paso Collaborative for Academic Excellence are two excellent examples of this stage in the model. Lieberman (2000) argues that because these types of organizations are "loose, borderless, and flexible," they are better suited than bureaucratic organizations to mobilize resources and initiatives for improving schools. She argues that because networks, collaboratives, and partnerships are "organized around the interests and needs of their participants," they are therefore more viable as the macro-level organizational structures for the professional development of teachers and preparation of candidates. It is not only the greater flexibility of networks, collaboratives, and coalitions that makes them significant in school reform. It is also that they create a new public space that brings together participants from all three levels of activity— micro (instructional), meso (professional), and macro (policy)—for a common set of purposes related to improving teaching, learning, and practice.

The nine qualities of an urban-focused, community-dedicated, and diversity-responsive school–university partnership explained in Chapter 1 provide a rough trajectory of development for creating the coalition or network of such partnerships necessary for producing community teachers and renewing urban schools.

SUMMARY POINTS

The CT framework can be summarized as follows:

1. The expectation that the largely White, middle-class, monolingual, culturally mainstream corps of potential teachers can become accomplished and culturally responsive urban teachers is not unrealistic, given the right conditions. The conditions are that of a practice-oriented, community-dedicated, and urban-focused program—the theme of this book.
2. The right social and cultural context must be constructed, one in which the authentic work of teachers and other educational professionals can be assisted and assessed.
3. A new notion of *practice* is necessary, one that underscores the fact that practice is not simply what one does, but rather is to be understood as some commonly recognizable knowledge-in-use that produces worthwhile results in students' academic achievement and personal development. The success of one's professional practice is dependent on the quality of one's knowledge-in-use.
4. In developing the trajectory of development in the program of study, considerable collaboration with community partners must be elicited by the school of education so that the cultural and historical components of people, communities, and neighborhoods are incorporated into the candidate's knowledge-in-practice. The entire trajectory of their development and transformation must be conceptualized and built into a curriculum.
5. Development of new contexts for collaborative work across sites, institutions, professions, disciplines, locations, and roles is essential. These new contexts are referred to as *circles of practice* and *communities of practice*. When they are small—determined by common specific enterprise in a common space (e.g., clinical triad and grade-level teams)—they are *circles of practice*. When they are larger—involving more individuals across institutions who share a number of interests, enterprises, or initiatives—they are called *communities of practice*.
6. Practice-oriented teacher education requires that candidates be engaged in *authentic work*. In contrast to merely observing classrooms—an experience that perhaps merely reinforces an acceptance of the very routines and practices that ought to be transformed—candidates need to be participants in meaningful pedagogy.

References

Abdal-Haqq, I. (1998). *Professional development schools: Weighing the evidence.* Thousand Oaks, CA: Corwin Press.

Adger, C. T., Christian, D., & Taylor, O. (Eds.). (1999). *Making the connection: Language and academic achievement among African American students.* McHenry, IL: Center for Applied Linguistics and Delta Systems Company.

American Federation of Teachers. (2000). *Building a profession: Strengthening teacher education and induction.* Washington, DC: Author.

Andrew, M. D. (1997). What matters most for teacher educators. *Journal of Teacher Education, 40*(5), 167–176.

Baugh, J. (1999). *Out of the mouths of slaves: African-American language and educational malpractice.* Austin: University of Texas Press.

Brown, S., Collins, A., & Duguid, P. (1989). Situated cognition and the culture of learning. *Educational Researcher, 18,* 32–42.

Cochran-Smith, M. (1996, April). *Constructing a knowledge base for urban teaching.* Presentation at the annual meeting of the American Educational Research Association, New York.

Comer, J. P. (1997). *Waiting for a miracle: Why schools can't solve our problems—and how we can.* New York: Dutton.

Comer, J., & Poussaint, A. F. (1992). *Raising Black children: Two leading psychiatrists confront the educational, social, and emotional problems facing Black children.* New York: Plume Books.

Council of Great City Schools. (1999). A survey of academic progress and promising practices in the great city schools: Preliminary report. http://www.cgcs.org.

Daniels, H. (1994). *Literature circles: Voice and choice in the student-centered classroom.* York, ME: Stenhouse.

Danielson, C. (1996). *Enhancing professional practice: A framework for teaching.* Alexandria, VA: Association for Supervision and Curriculum Development.

Darling-Hammond, L. (1992). *Standards of practice for learner-centered schools.* New York: National Center for Restructuring Education, Schools, and Teaching.

Darling-Hammond, L. (Ed.). (1994). *Professional development schools: Schools for developing a profession.* New York: Teachers College Press.

Darling-Hammond, L. (1997). *The right to learn: A blueprint for creating schools that work.* San Francisco: Jossey-Bass.

Darling-Hammond, L., & Sykes, G. (Eds.). (1999). *Teaching as the learning profession: Handbook of policy and practice.* San Francisco: Jossey-Bass.

Delpit, L. D. (1996). *Other people's children: Cultural conflict in the classroom.* Toronto: University of Toronto Press.

Dewey, J. (1933). *How we think: A restatement of the relation of reflective thinking to the educative process.* Boston: Henry Holt.

Diez, M. E. (1990). A thrust from within: Reconceptualizing teacher education at Alverno college. *Peabody Journal of Education, 65*(2), 4–18.

Diez, M., & Hass, J. M. (1997). No more piecemeal reform: Using performance-based approaches to rethink teacher education. *Action in Teacher Education, 19*(2), 17–26.

Diez, M., Rickards, W. H., & Lake, K. (1994). In T. Warren (Ed.), *Promising practices: Teacher education in liberal arts colleges* (pp. 9–18). New York: University Press of America.

Elmore, R. F. (1996). Getting to scale with good educational practice. *Harvard Educational Review, 66*(1), 1–26.

Epstein, J. L., Sanders, M. G., & Clark, L. A. (1999). *Preparing educators for school–family–community partnerships: Results of a national survey of colleges and universities* (Report No. 34). Baltimore: Johns Hopkins University Center for Research on the Education of Students Placed at Risk.

Foster, M. (1997). *Black teachers on teaching.* New York: New Press.

Galambos, J. A., Abelson, R. P., & Black, J. B. (Eds.). (1986). *Knowledge structures.* Hillsdale, NJ: Erlbaum.

Goodlad, J. (1994). *Education renewal: Better teachers, better schools.* San Francisco: Jossey-Bass.

Griffin, G. (1999). Changes in teacher education: Looking to the future. In G. Griffin & M. Early (Eds.), *The education of teachers: Ninety-eighth yearbook of the National Society for the Study of Education.* Chicago: University of Chicago Press.

Hargreaves, A. (1994). *Changing teachers, changing times: Teachers' work and culture in the postmodern age.* New York: Teachers College Press.

Hargreaves, A., & Fullan, M. (1996). *What's worth fighting for in your school?* New York: Teachers College Press.

Hoffman, J. V., Bauman, J. F., Afflerbach, P., Duffy-Hester, A. M., McCarthey, S. J., & Ro, J. M. (2000). *Balancing principles for teaching elementary reading.* Mahwah, NJ: Erlbaum.

Hollins, E. R., King, J. E., & Hayman, W. C. (Eds.). (1994). *Teaching diverse populations: Formulating the knowledge base.* Albany, NY: State University of New York Press.

Holmes Group. (1986). *Tomorrow's schools of education.* East Lansing, MI: Author.

Holmes Group. (1990). *Tomorrow's schools: Principles for the design of professional development schools.* East Lansing, MI: Author.

Hymes, D. (1974). *The foundations of sociolinguistics: Sociolinguistic ethnography.* Philadelphia: University of Pennsylvania Press.

Irvine, J. J., & Fraser, J. (1998). Warm demanders: Do national certification standards leave room from the culturally responsive pedagogy of African American teachers? *Education Week, 17*(3), 42, 56.

King, J. E. (1991). Dysconscious racism: Ideology, identity, and miseducation of teachers. *Journal of Negro Eeducation, 69*(2), 133–146.

Kozol, J. (1991). *Savage inequalities.* New York: Crown.

Kunjufu, J. (1996). *Countering the conspiracy to destroy Black boys.* Chicago: African American Images. (Original work published 1983)

Labaree, D. F., & Pallas, A. M. (1996). Dire straits: The narrow vision of the Holmes Group. *Educational Researcher, 25*(4), 25–28.

Labov, W. (1972). *Language in the inner city: Studies in the Black English vernacular.* Philadelphia: University of Pennsylvania Press.

Ladson-Billings, G. (1994). *The dreamkeepers: Successful teachers of African American children.* San Francisco: Jossey-Bass.

Lave, J. (1988). *Cognition in practice: Mind, mathematics, and culture in everyday life.* Cambridge, UK: Cambridge University Press.

Lave, J., & Wenger, E. (1991). *Situated learning: Legitimate peripheral participation.* Cambridge, UK: Cambridge University Press.

Lee, C. D. (1994). African-centered pedagogy: Complexities and possibilities. In M. J. Shujaa (Ed.), *Too much schooling, too little education: A paradox in Black life in White societies* (pp. 295–318). Trenton, NJ: African World Press.

Lieberman, A. (2000). Networks as learning communities: Shaping the future of teacher development. *Journal of Teacher Education, 51*(3), 221–233.

Liston, D. P., & Zeichner, K.M. (1991). *Teacher education and the social conditions of schooling.* New York: Routledge.

Lortie, D. C. (1975). *Schoolteacher: A sociological study.* Chicago: University of Chicago Press.

Meier, T. (1982). Personal communication.

Melnick, S. L., & Zeichner, K. M. (1997). *Enhancing the capacity of teacher education institutions to address diversity issues.* In J. E. King, E. R. Hollins, & W. C. Hayman (Eds.), Preparing teachers for cultural diversity (pp. 23–39). New York: Teachers College Press.

Miller, W. (1995). *Frederick Douglass: The last days of slavery.* New York: Lee and Low Books.

Miner, B. (1998). Embracing Ebonics and teaching standard English: An interview with Carrie Secret. In T. Perry and L. Delpit (Eds.), *The real Ebonics debate: Power, language and the education of African American children* (pp. 79–88). Boston: Beacon.

Murrell, P. C., Jr. (1991). Cultural politics in teacher education: What's missing in the preparation of African-American teachers? In M. Foster (Ed.), *Readings on equal education* (Vol. 11; pp. 205–225).

Murrell, P. C., Jr. (1993). Afrocentric immersion: Academic and personal development of African American males in public schools. In T. Perry & J. W. Fraser (Eds.), *Freedom's plow: Teaching in the multicultural classroom* (pp. 231–260). New York: Routledge.

Murrell, P. C., Jr. (1997). Digging again the family wells: A Freirean literacy framework as emancipatory pedagogy for African American children. In P. Freire, J. Fraser, D. Macedo, T. McKinnon, & W. Stokes (Eds.), *Mentoring the mentor: A critical dialog with Paulo Freire.* Albany: State University of New York Press.

Murrell, P. (1998). *Like stone soup: The role of the professional development school in the renewal of urban schools.* Washington, DC: American Association of Colleges of Teacher Education.

Murrell, P. C., Jr. (in press). *African-centered pedagogy: Building schools of achievement for African American children.* Albany: State University of New York Press.

Murrell, P.C., Jr., & Borunda, M. (1998). The cultural and community politics of educational equity: Toward a new framework of professional development schools. In N. J. Lauter (Ed.), *Professional development schools: Confronting realities* (pp. 65–86). New York: National Center for Restructuring Education, Schools and Teaching (NCREST).

Murrell, P. C., Jr., & Diez, M. E. (1997). Educating teachers for diversity: A teacher preparation program model for preparing multiculturally expert teachers. In E. Hollins, W. Hayman, & J. King (Eds.), *Meeting the challenge of diversity in teacher preparation* (pp. 113–145). New York: Teachers College Press.

Myers, C. B. (1996a, April). *Beyond the PDS: Schools* as *professional learning communities. A proposal based on an analysis of PDS efforts of the 1990's.* Paper presented at the annual meeting of the American Educational Research Association, New York.

Myers, C. B. (1996b, April). *University–school collaborations: A need to reconceptualize schools as professional learning communities instead of partnerships.* Paper presented at the annual meeting of the American Educational Research Association, New York.

National Center for Restructuring Education, Schools, and Teaching (NCREST). (2001). http://www.tc.columbia.edu/~ncrest/.

National Commission on Teaching and America's Future (NCTAF). (1996). *What matters most: Teaching for America's future:* New York: Carnegie Corporation and Rockefeller Foundation.

National Council for Accreditation of Teacher Education (NCATE). (2000). *Professional standards for the accreditation of schools, colleges and departments of education.* Washington, DC: Author.

Nias, J., Southworth, G., & Yeomans, R. (1989). *Staff relations in the primary school.* London: Cassell.

Nieto, S. (1999). *The light in their eyes: Creating multicultural learning communities.* New York: Teachers College Press.

Nieto, S. (2000). Placing equity front and center: Some thoughts on transforming teacher education for a new century. *Journal of Teacher Education, 51*(3), 180–187.

Oakes, J. (1985). *Keeping track: How schools structure inequality.* New Haven, CT: Yale University Press.

Obidah, J. E., & Teel, K. M. (2001). *Because of the kids.* New York: Teachers College Press.

Ogbu, J. (1992). Understanding cultural diversity and learning. *Educational Researcher, 21*(8), 5–14.

Orfield, G., Bachmeier, M. D., James, D. R., & Eitle, T. (1997, April). *Deepening segregation in American public schools.* Cambridge, MA: Harvard Project on School Desegregation.

Patterson, R. S., Michelli, N. M., & Pacheco, A. (1999). *Centers of pedagogy: New structures of educational renewal.* San Francisco: Jossey-Bass.

Peshkin, A. (2000). The nature of interpretation in qualitative research. *Educational Researcher, 29*(9), 5–9.

Piestrup, A. M. (1973). *Black dialect interference and accommodation of reading instruction in the first grade* (Monographs of the Language Behavior Research Laboratory No. 4). Berkeley: University of California Press.

Rickford, J. R. (1999). *African American vernacular English.* Malden, MA: Blackwell.

Rickford, J. R., & Rickford, R. J. (2000). *Spoken soul: The story of Black English.* New York: Wiley.

Sarason, S. (1971). *The culture of the school and the problem of change* (2nd ed.). Boston: Allyn & Bacon.

Schön, D. A. (1989). *Educating the reflective practitioner: Toward a new design for teaching and learning.* San Francisco: Jossey-Bass.

Senge, P. (1995). *The fifth discipline: The art and practice of learning organization.* New York: Dooubleday.

Shirley, D. (1997). *Community organizing for urban school reform.* Austin: University of Texas Press.

Shujaa, M. J. (1994). Education and schooling: Can you have one without the other? In M. J. Shujaa (Ed.), *Too much schooling, too little education: A paradox in Black life in White societies* (pp. 13–36). Trenton, NJ: African World Press.

Sizer, T. R. (1992). *Horace's compromise: The dilemma of the American high school.* Boston: Houghton Mifflin.

Smitherman, G. (1986). *Talkin and testifyin: The language of Black America.* Detroit: Wayne State University Press. (Original work published 1977)

Spring, J. (1990). *The American school: 1642–1990* (2nd ed.). New York: Longman.

Steele, C. (1997). A threat in the air. *American Psychologist, 52*(6), 613–629.

Sykes, G. (1997). Worthy of the name: Standards for the professional development school. In M. Levine & R. Trachtman (Eds.), *Building professional development schools: Politics, practice and policy* (pp. 159–193). New York: Teachers College Press.

Tatum, B. D. (1992). Talking about race, learning about racism: The implication of racial identity development theory in the classroom. *Harvard Educational Review, 62*(1), 1–24.

Tharp, R. G., & Gallimore, R. (1991). *Rousing minds to life: Teaching learning and schooling in social context.* Cambridge, UK: Cambridge University Press.

Tom, A. R. (1997). *Redesigning teacher education.* Albany: State University of New York Press.

Triesman, P. U. (1985). *A study of mathematics achievement of Black students at the University of California, Berkeley.* Unpublished doctoral dissertation, University of California, Berkeley.

Valli, L., Cooper, D., & Frankes, L. (1997). Professional development schools and equity: A critical analysis of rhetoric and research. In M. W. Apple (Ed.), *Review of research in education: Vol. 22* (pp. 251–304). Washington, DC: American Educational Research Association.

Vavrus, M. (1995). Tomorrow's schools of education: The Holmes Group. *Educational Studies, 26*(1/2), 135–139.

Wenger, E. (1999). *Communities of practice: Learning, meaning and identity.* Cambridge, UK: Cambridge University Press.

Wiggins, G., & McTighe, J. (1998). *Understanding by design.* Alexandria, VA: Association for Supervision and Curriculum Development.

Williams, B. (Ed.). (1999). *Closing the achievement gap: A vision for changing beliefs and practices.* Alexandria, VA: Association for Supervision as Curricula Development.

Wiske, M. S. (1998). *Teaching for understanding: Linking research with practice.* San Francisco: Jossey-Bass.

Woodson, C. G. (1990). *The miseducation of the Negro.* Washington, DC: Africa World Press. (Original work published 1933)

Yon, D. A. (2000). *Elusive culture: Schooling, race, and identity in global times.* Albany: State University of New York Press.

Zeichner, K. M. (1996). Educating teachers to close the achievement gap: Issues of pedagogy, knowledge and teacher preparation. In B. Williams (Ed.), *Closing the achievement gap: A vision for changing beliefs and practices* (pp. 56–76). Alexandria, VA: Association for Supervision and Curriculum Development.

Zernike, K. (2000, August 24). Less training, more teachers: New math for staffing classes. *New York Times.*

Index

About the Author

Peter C. Murrell, Jr., is an associate professor of urban education at Northeastern University in Boston, Massachusetts, where he also directs the Center for Innovation in Urban Education. He received his Ph.D. in Urban Education (educational psychology) from the University of Wisconsin–Milwaukee, specializing in human learning and cognition. He earned his M.S. degree from the University of Wisconsin–Madison in experimental psychology, specializing in cognition and learning, and his B.A. in psychology from Carleton College in Northfield, Minnesota, where he graduated with honors.

Peter Murrell currently teaches graduate and undergraduate courses in cognitive psychology, learning and cognition, and the social contexts of urban teaching. He has been a teacher and researcher in urban school reform for the last two decades, including teaching at the middle school, high school, and postsecondary levels. His professional work is in the development of exemplary urban teachers through community-based and practice-oriented teacher preparation in Boston, Massachusetts. His research interests are in qualitative studies of human learning in cultural and community context. He has received a Distinguished Scholastic Achievement Award for Black Scholarship in New England.

Dr. Murrell is the author of the recent monograph *Like Stone Soup: The Role of the Professional Development School in the Renewal of Urban Schools* and has written numerous journal articles and book chapters on urban teaching and learning. He is currently completing work on a book on effective pedagogy for African American children entitled *African-Centered Pedagogy: Developing Schools of Achievement for African American Children* (State University of New York Press).